UNCUT

Raw Unadulterated Stories of Addiction

KIMBER LYNNE

Copyright © Kimber Lynne 2020

All rights reserved. No part of this publication may be reproduced, stored in a retrieval system, or transmitted in any form or by any means, mechanical, photocopying, recording or otherwise, without prior permission in writing of the author.

ISBN: 9798643291978 (paperback)
Imprint: Independently published

About the Author

Kimber Lynne has been a broadcast journalist since the early 80's. For the past 10 years alcohol and drug addiction within her own family has created a passion for helping others who are dealing with the disease. After two years of interviewing recovering addicts, parents of addicts, pharmacist, pain management doctors, law enforcement coupled with her own experiences she has put together the best of the transcripts in hopes that others can better understand opioid addiction in an effort to help their loved ones.

TOGETHER WE NEED TO BURY THE CONSPIRACY OF <u>SILENCE</u>.

As a broadcast journalist, I have had the opportunity to interview recovering addicts who deliver gripping details of their arduous journey fighting addiction. My passion for wanting to do this stemmed from my personal journey with one of my children whose addiction affected our immediate family and those closest to us. As a result, I am more sympathetic to the disease and have a better understanding of how an addict, once hooked, can't just say no. "UnCut" is to help families, loved ones, and anyone who has been or is being touched by opioid addiction. This transcript will help the reader better understand the cycle of addiction from initial use to rehabilitation. In the event drug use is suspected or confirmed, one will also find resources for help. The interviews are real and, at times, hard to comprehend. The names have been changed to protect recovery and anonymity of those who participated in telling their story.

This book is dedicated to Eddie Kaplan. My friend and colleague who knew the grip of opioid addiction and was committed to making a difference.

No one becomes an addict by choice. Addiction happens over time, and not everyone who uses will become an addict. Addicts are not terrible people. If you haven't already heard this from a friend or colleague, you will. By reading "Uncut," you will have the tools to properly respond to such comments as, "Well, you know it's a choice."

Prologue

I have been personally affected by addiction, which enabled me to ask the appropriate questions to those that appear in this book.

There will not be any type of medical explanations or hardcore statistics mentioned here. This book is strictly first-person accounts of dealing with addiction from those that lived the nightmare and by those who have dealt with a loved one with the addiction.

Everyone knows someone who suffers from some type of addiction. It may be sugar. It could be exercise. In many cases, it is food or work or shopping. The difference between these "accepted" addictions and what the world is dealing with today is what is known as acceptable behavior. The addictions mentioned above generally are not looked down upon by society. They are acceptable behavior. Opioid and alcohol abuse carries a stigma of bad behavior and is associated as a moral weakness or a willful choice.

1

ADDICTION IS NOT A SOLO FLIGHT

▲ ▲ ▲

"Honest to God, I had the sensation to go in and get a plastic bag and put over your head and let you run out of air and then bury you."

▲ ▲ ▲

Timothy was the most powerful interview I recorded. Honestly, his entire interview was captivating. He is a recovered addict from the '70s who years later experienced the ultimate loss of his daughter who died from a heroin overdose. In this chapter, I will set you up with how Timothy and other parents who I interviewed saw the addiction and what they tried to do to get their child through it. Be mindful that these are raw transcripts and not edited for correct grammar.

> *Kimber Lynne:* You knew it was wrong. You crossed that line just a little bit too much, and you knew you were in trouble. So, what makes a kid at that age (16) do that?

Timothy: It's all society, what society expects. You're expected to be popular, pretty, just athletically superior. And, if you're not any of those, you have a problem with who you are. There's a problem with who you are if you're not in one of those categories. And a way to feel all right with yourself, to feel something outside of what you're actually feeling is drugs. If you feel ugly, if you feel fat, if you're not as athletic, you feel slow if you don't fit in. You know, there was a drug crowd. You could always fit in with them. You get high, it made you not feel inadequate, and everything was fine.

Kimber Lynne: It's a temporary fix?

Timothy: It was a temporary fix but a fix, nonetheless. So, you always seek that fix. You know, what if I feel fat today? I get high, and I don't feel fat, and it wears off, I feel fat again. Get high again; keep it going. That's where the problems start.

Kimber Lynne: When do you know it's an addiction and not just recreation?

Timothy: When the day comes that you really don't want to do it, but you do it anyway.

▲▲▲

Timothy was an addict in the '70s, and his fight continued off and on even when his daughter was conceived. His story is pertinent in helping families understand what they are dealing with. I know from personal experience that it takes a long time to uncover the seriousness of addiction. I would say, as a non-addict, it is a battle of denial and really not wanting to believe that this could happen in your own family. Timothy had an inside track and still couldn't see his own daughter's path to destruction.

Kimber Lynne: When did you first know she was dabbling. And one more thing, did she know your story?

Timothy: Oh, she knew my story because I got clean for four years, and she was probably about six years old now. And for some reason I decided, as addition goes, I was doing well. I could drink a beer, and it would lead me right back to addiction. I tried hiding all that. And then at six years old, she (his daughter) was starting to pick up on things like Mom's crying a lot at night. Dad's missing a lot when he's not supposed to be. She was a smart girl, and she started picking up that something was off.

▲ ▲ ▲

When you are a parent, and you provide opportunities for your children to be successful, you never in your wildest dreams believe that they will ever turn to drugs or become an addict. Timothy's daughter was an honor roll student and musically gifted, so you would think there is absolutely no reason to worry. Right?

Timothy: At about 16, she did something just way out of character. Like told a lie, or something. It's way out of character. I had some years clean and when she did what she did, something in me, I saw it. I was like, that's an addict. I saw me. I said that's something I would do. That's something I did that when I was lying. I was getting high. I just saw that in her and something inside me was like, oh God, oh God, please don't let her be like me, like that. I was like, if that's what's going on, I did this. I planted some evil in her.

▲ ▲ ▲

Pay attention to the lies. Pay attention to the lies. Pay attention to the lies. You know deep down that it's a lie. You ask a question, and you don't get an answer that makes any sense at all. Addicts are master manipulators. They say and do whatever it takes to get what they want. Here is where most parents make the early mistake of enabling the addiction.

Like Timothy, Alan is a parent who suffered emotionally and financially with his child. Thousands and thousands of dollars and many, many years later, he was able to find strength in exercising the toughest love possible. Unlike Timothy, Alan did not have the understanding of "using" to gauge the seriousness of what was ahead.

Kimber Lynne: Talk to me about the lies, lying.

Alan: It was easier to lie. My daughter could tell some of the best lies. She would lie about the lie. There was two things that my daughter had become is a liar and a thief, and she was proficient at both. And I find out that most people like her are really good liars and really good thieves because I feel like you're not dealing with your daughter or son anymore. It's like something has taken over their body. The body is there, but the child that she once knew is not.

Kimber Lynne: Was there anger in the house as you were trying to figure all this out?

Alan: Yeah, my wife, not so much. Me a lot because I didn't understand it. Sometimes I'd yell and scream and tell her really what I thought about her. I find out through Celebrate Recovery you shouldn't do that, but you know you have to. You sometimes have to express yourself, or you feel like you're going to explode inside.

Kimber Lynne: They'll get to a certain point where they can't feel normal anymore. They wake up looking for a fix so that they can sit at a table much like we are now and hold a conversation. You know something big is going on, but you don't have hardcore proof.

Alan: Yeah, sure. We'd always threatened with a drug test, and of course, we actually got one, couldn't get her to take it. It was always a lie, or I've got to go here and go there, and you would see her not out, and she would leave and come back. And 15-20 minutes later she seemed to be if you want to call it – normal. She was more alert because she had gotten the drugs, and at that time, it was opioids. She hadn't switched over to heroin at that time.

Kimber Lynne: Did you ever find proof?

Timothy: I went in her room, scrounged around, I saw a box. A box about yay big like what you get from the pharmacist when you buy hypodermic needles. You get a box of them, and she hadn't hidden it. They get a little sloppy. I come to notice these little, like, specks on the wall. It was spatters of blood where they shoot up and hit a vein. And I grabbed this box and my heart sunk. I was like, oh my God. She's shooting up. I was like, oh my God. And I grabbed the box, and I open it. It's new syringes, used syringes, there's a spoon, bent burnt marks, pieces of cotton in it with blood. I saw baggies, little powder in it. I saw a bunch of extra baggies for bagging up to sell. I'm like, oh my God. I started to relive the failure all over again. I was like, I can't do this anymore. As much as I love this girl, she's 27 years old now when this happened, as much as I love her. I just can't do it anymore. I'm just enabling her to just keep doing it. I'm hurting her more than helping her.

Kimber Lynne: When it gets to a point where the parents are figuring out enough not to give them money, or they're saying I'm cutting you off, that's when they can't afford the $80 a pill on the street anymore. Is that when they cross that line?

Alan: That's correct. I sat in with our sheriff and expressed all these problems that I was having, and I said, "She's lost her job, and she's trying to get money any way she can, she's stealing and so forth. And he told me, he said, "Now here's what's going to happen to your daughter. Your daughter is going to come to the conclusion she can't afford the opioids and heroin is much, much cheaper." And a month later, she made that transition.

Kimber Lynne: When you found out, how scared were you?

Alan: Very. She was not any good to herself. She was not any good to us. She stole. You're so very, very tired. Excuse me *(tearing up)* that you feel like that she would be better off dead. And a lot of parents I've talked to had said this, and I let my daughter move back in with me. And she was sitting out on the patio, and she's nodding out. She had left and gone out and got heroin and came back. The audacity of her sitting on my patio doing drugs. I've told her later on, I said, "Honest to God, I had the sensation to go in and get a plastic bag and put over your head and let you run out of air, and then bury you." She said, "That was awful," I said, "You don't know where I was coming from. The stress on us is awful."

▲ ▲ ▲

If you are in the middle of this "hell," then you know that every waking moment you are trying to make sense of what is happening in your family. You are reading every piece of literature you can put your hands on. You are wanting to talk to others, but the stigma that is associated with having a child that is a drug addict forces you to keep everything bottled up inside. The part that you are unprepared for is when you finally leave the denial stage of believing that it can't be as bad as what you hear on the news to; it is that bad. That is when the real nightmare begins – sleepless nights upon sleepless nights. Then there is the anguish of trying to decipher between a real "need" or a ploy to gain money to buy drugs? The countless phone calls asking to borrow money. The plea for food because they haven't eaten in two days. Then, I don't have gas to get to work. On and on it goes until you find the strength to stop enabling. To make the decision that you won't give any more money because deep down, you know the fifty dollars you wire transferred, or the twenty dollars cash you deposited into an account, *(because*

Kimber Lynne

cash makes the funds immediately available) could be the drug money that causes an overdose. So, at this moment, you have to let this disease take its course. You pray, and then you pray again. You beg God to save your child. You pray that the phone call – yes, THAT phone call never comes.

Kimber Lynne: Were you estranged from her when she Od'd?

Timothy: Yeah.

Kimber Lynne: So, tell me about that day

Timothy: That day, well, a week prior, my wife was still going to see our daughter in jail. Ebony was in our city jail a lot, and my wife was going to see her and stuff. And my wife had arranged for her to go from jail to a treatment center. I was like, okay. I'm not going to go visit her in jail; I'm not doing that. I love her, but it hurts me too much to even, I think I saw her once. And I hugged her, and she looked like she was just out of it, and I couldn't even bear to see her like that. She was in jail soon to be in a treatment center.

Here's what happened. Our daughter was good with hooking up with the big-time dope dealers. And people would come and bail her out of jail so she could be back with the crew to score to get dope. She liked to play the game, and she was good at it, and we wanted her to get out of jail and go to treatment. They had bailed her out to get her on the streets. So, the last thing I heard was that she was in jail. I was just like, she's in the Lord's hand because I just, I've got another kid, I just can't deal with this. She's in the Lord's hands – let it go. So, she's in jail. One night, it's August 2017, 2:30 in the morning I get a phone call. I'm thinking, the whole time in your mind you're thinking, like, please God rescue her from this addiction before it kills her, please. I get a phone call, 2:30 in the morning. Nobody calls me at 2:30 in the morning, nobody. I'm like, hello? Is this Timothy? Yeah. Is your daughter (name)? I'm thinking, oh God, she got arrested or something; what has she done. Why are you calling me?

She's 27. I'm like, yeah, she's my daughter. Okay, sir, I'm the medical examiner. Right then, I started hearing a loud ringing in my ear and my mind just, you know, my mind just started really tripping around I'm like, you know, a still ring. I was like, yeah. He said, your daughter is deceased. I kind of blanked out. It was kind of like a loud ringing. I put the phone down. I'm like; I didn't just hear that. I didn't just hear that.

▲ ▲ ▲

A parent's worst nightmare. The call all of us hope we never get. Timothy had the knowledge of addictive behavior. He already knew his daughter was using and dealing toxic drugs. He and his wife were doing all the right things trying to save her. Bottom-line is the only way an addict receives help is if they want it. Nothing you can say will make them want to get clean. As a parent, what you are going through is just hell. It's hell in the house. It's you, wondering what you did wrong raising them. I've even heard parents writing a letter to their child and making them read it because having a conversation just escalates into an argument. You ask them, "What did we do wrong?" Was this your friends we let you hang out with? Do you not love us? And then you get to the point that you just want the nightmare over with. You are tired, and you just want it over.

Kimber Lynne: How many years did it go on? You got to that point, and you did something they call "tough love." Your daughter had crossed the line from opioids (pills) to shooting heroin. You crossed the line when you said, "I'm willing to let her die." Talk about the strength you needed so that other parents reading this can understand. How do you get to that point where you say, "I'm going to make a decision here, and when I make it, it's going to be the hardest decision I ever made because now I'm saying, I'm willing to lose her."?

Alan: You got to do it quickly, and most parents don't. I was fortunate enough to talk to a lot of right people and it was like every day I was out searching for information and you find that you better do it quick. The only thing I would let her continue to have was her cell phone, but I wouldn't buy her anything. And it got so bad to the point that I'd had enough. I told her, I said, "You get out of my house." I said, "I don't care where you go." I said, "But you need to put a little note in your pocket that if you die of an overdose, I will not even honor you to bury you in my family cemetery. They can do with you whatever they do with derelict bodies." I mean, you're, you're crazy. You're tired, and she said, "Well, I won't even go to your funeral." I said, "At this point in time, you're not going to be able to, you'll be dead." So, she left and she went to a friend in New Jersey, which was a drug addict and stayed there for several months. And called back and said, "I've had enough. Can I come home?" I said, "Absolutely not." She said, "Well, where am I going to sleep?" I said, "Don't care. Try a bench or somewhere under a tree, I don't care. You're not coming here. I've had it with you. You're not the person; you're not my daughter any longer. Somebody else is in your body." So she ended up calling a friend that was in rehab with her that had made it through the rehab, and he said, "Well, you can stay here one day," He said, "And I'm going to call around and then you've got to take these telephone numbers, and you go get a place in a halfway house." So, she came back, spent one night with them and then they left and she stayed in the halfway house for about a year or so. So, if you had to be tough and if you don't get there quickly, you usually don't have a second chance.

Kimber Lynne: Your biggest fear now?

Alan: That she'll be like a lot of other people that we've had in our groups that one day she'll pick it up and do it again and think she can start where she left off, and it'll kill her.

▲ ▲ ▲

Just about every parent I interviewed had similar stories of behavior and consistent confrontation of trying to get their child to wake up and stop. But as the story goes, you will learn that a request such as that can't happen in a short-term environment. Furthermore, not one story had a positive outcome after a 28-day treatment facility. Many times, it was because the addict succumbed to the pressure and agreed to go solely to satisfy the family or a significant other and the family believed 28 days would fix the problem. Every single addict I interviewed, relapsed almost immediately after returning from a 28-day program. Bill is a parent whose daughter spent years in and out of treatment facilities. He endured overdoses and supported his daughter through jail time.

Kimber Lynne

Bill: She was clean for about almost a year and a half. After she came out, it seemed like she was really trying but then all of a sudden, she disappeared again. She would go without telling us where she was and stuff like that.

Kimber Lynne: Did your heart start sinking again when that happened?

Bill: We were so proud of her when she lasted as long as she did you know. And then come to find out she's back doing it. Just like oh my God, I can't believe this. You know, what do we have to do? I mean is jail not enough. Going off for 28 days is that not enough? What's next and we thought Jesus maybe we should get some social group involved, maybe we should get her more involved in church. Maybe we should go ahead and tell the police – get her arrested. Whatever we need to do.

▲ ▲ ▲

The deceit is the nasty truth about the journey. Next, we will hear straight from the addicts. How it started? When it turned from recreation to addiction. Why they continued, where they scored the drugs? Who they became?

2

THE PATH TO ADDICTION

▲▲▲

"I went like from this innocent kid that would never do drugs to this full blown junkie that was stealing from my family that loved me the most and not caring if I lived or died."

▲▲▲

Be prepared to be enlightened. You may start seeing your child's story play out in these interviews. Also know that these encounters are probably very similar to what your son, daughter or loved one has or is experiencing. I wish I didn't know now what I didn't know then. That's the ugly reality of being part of the addiction statistic. Through it all, we will be able to help someone else through their journey.

Kimber Lynne: You're 23? When did it start for you?

Jill: When did I start using?

Kimber Lynne: Yes.

Jill: Well, I started using when I was 16, originally. I think it got really difficult. I was a full-blown addict when I was 19. It was when I started using opiates, and it was pretty much all downhill from there.

Kimber Lynne: Who convinced you? "Hey, just try this. It's no big deal."

Jill: No-one had to convince me. I mean, I heard it was good and…

Kimber Lynne: That was enough for you?

Jill: Yeah. I mean, I was 10 feet tall and bulletproof. I knew everything at 18…I thought I did. I enjoyed a party. I enjoyed feeling good. I guess the first time that I tried opiates; I can remember, specifically, the first time I started snorting opiates because that was my way, that was my thing. It was a girlfriend of mine. I mean, she was my best friend, and I trusted her. I thought she wouldn't put me in a situation that would be dangerous or change my life the way that it did. So, I didn't think twice the first time that I snorted a pill. I didn't think this is a bad idea. This might end up taking everything from me. It was just; I'm gonna feel good. This is gonna be fun. I'm gonna party, and it's going to be great.

Kimber Lynne: Growing up, I know I've said it to my kids where it's like, "Hey, just say no." Drugs are bad. Don't do that." Did you have any fear? Any, I don't want to disappoint my parents? They say it destroys lives. I mean, you had to have heard that at a younger age.

Jill: Yeah, of course, just say no. I mean, I was rebellious. All the time, my parents said, "Just say no," that was me, "Just say yes." I'm truthfully; I think that as a kid, or as a young teen, there's nothing that you could've said to me. Even if you looked right at me and told me, "In five years, your life's gonna be this way because of what you're doing right now." I don't think I would've believed you. I don't think it would've made a difference at all, really.

Kimber Lynne: You take that first pill, and it's a prescription. It's regulated by the FDA. Makes you feel good. Probably not costing you too much money at this particular point. Probably took it out of a cabinet or someone gave it to you. You're still not suffering financially or probably physically at this point. Then tell me what happens.

Jill: Well, truthfully, I have never taken a pill from someone's medicine cabinet. I got them from the street originally. I mean they were already on the street by the time… when I was using them. I mean, that's not necessarily true. I guess the first…if we'll talk very specifically, okay the first Percocet that I used, it was a 5 milligram Percocet. And it was from my boyfriend's Mom's dresser drawer. She took them for her neck or something. They made me sick. I threw up. It was terrible. I took two and I hated it. But then, as my tolerance grew, I had to continue to take more in order to feel that same good feeling. So, it escalated from a simple Perc 5, which is something that you would get for a very simple procedure, it's very mild. I mean, it's pretty regular, to a Percocet 30, which is, from what I understand and I'm not super medically educated, but it's something that you would get if you had a terminal illness. They are almost pure. It's like prescription heroin really because it's an almost pure opiate. There isn't all of that Tylenol and aspirin that goes into the lower milligrams to dilute the actual opiate. So, it was as if I was shooting heroin, but it was safer. It wasn't as addicting, so I thought. So, I'd been told. That's the way the story goes.

Kimber Lynne: The more you take, the more you need to feel normal, which people don't understand?

Jill: Right.

▲ ▲ ▲

For me, we always tried to put our kids in the best environment possible. Made sure they were active in after school activities. Made sure they went to church. We sent them to private school so that we could give them the best early education and somewhat control their friendships. My husband and I were very active in their childhood activities. We coached, we hosted the overnight sleepovers, we monitored their academic successes and failures. We gave them every opportunity to be the best they could be. What I know now is that all that doesn't matter if a child has the predisposition and the chemical makeup that puts them at risk of addiction. Short of putting them in lockdown until they get past a certain age, you won't be able to spend every minute of every day micromanaging their life. Diane was also a child who came from a very loving family and had all the morals and character traits of someone that you never would have expected to go down this road that changed her life forever.

Diane: I was 18 years old. It was the summer that I got out of high school that I really started kind of dabbling in drugs. I was always one of those people that was way against it. Even, you know, smoking weed. Everything, forever. I had a friend growing up that her brother was, you know, he was into heroin and I watched her struggle, and him struggle and he ended up losing his life. So, I was always one of those people that, you know, drugs are bad. I'd never get involved in that kind of thing, and I had a good upbringing. I had good morals. I had wonderful parents. So, the fact that I started doing what I was doing was insane.

Kimber Lynne: You have a friend who loses her brother. That's a big deal, and it wasn't like you got into a bad crowd in high school. That you were, like, hanging out with bad kids, smoking outback, doing all that stuff. How does one cross that line?

Diane: As soon as I got out of high school, I dated this guy that, you know, he smoked weed, and I was never about that. That was never me, but they were always doing it around me, and I don't know. I just wasn't really great with the whole peer pressure thing. So, I tried it, and I didn't really like it. So, I didn't do it for a while, and it just was around me, and I loved this guy. So, I tried it again, and, eventually, I kind of liked it. So, when I got out of high school, and I started dating, you know, the guy that I'm originally talking about, this wonderful guy. I fell hard for him, but I didn't know exactly everything that he was involved in. It was kind of too late. I was already really attached, and I don't know. I just felt safe with him. So, it started out just at a party having fun with everybody. All of our friends and somebody had a Vicodin and was like, "Here, try this." And I was already kind of drinking-ish, so I was like okay.

I tried it, and I liked the way it made me feel. So, that kind of broke the barrier, I guess, but it was still, you know, it wasn't the whole doing heroin thing that my friend's brother died from. So, I don't know. I just kind of thought I could control it. Well, I was wrong. What happened, basically, was I had no idea that he had a full-blown addiction that I didn't know about. It would turn from a party, to like, the weekends to like, a couple days a week, you know? And then, it was full-fledged.

Kimber Lynne: You weren't aware that it was going to be something you couldn't just stop doing?

Diane: I realized one day, I just didn't want to do it anymore. It was just like, I don't want to do it. I just don't have the desire to and that was when I realized that he had this full-blown addiction because it became not an option for me anymore. My relationship became emotionally, verbally and physically abusive. So, I was forced to sell everything I had and buy drugs. Sorry, it's kind of hard to talk about. One thing led to another, and basically, it was a total of six months of me having fun and you know, just playing around.

And before I knew it, I had a full-blown addiction that I couldn't control. I went from this innocent kid that would never do drugs to this full-blown junkie that was stealing from my family that loved me the most and not caring if I lived or died.

▲ ▲ ▲

I can't tell you how many times I heard as my family was battling this drug addiction *(alcohol addiction was also present with family members)*, that it was a choice; that it is a choice that they are using or drinking. During the two years of interviews I have discovered that some people became addicted because of wisdom teeth extraction or some minor surgery that the doctor prescribed pain meds to help with recovery. Yes, for most, at first, it is a choice that ultimately becomes a need and we will get into why they need the substance in later chapters. It is something that you have to come to grips with if you are genuinely going to be in a situation to help your loved ones through this. Chayne wasn't as fortunate in deciding whether to experiment or not. The cards were stacked against him almost from the beginning.

Kimber Lynne: When did you start using drugs for the very first time?

Chayne: The very first time I drank alcohol, I was three years old. Yeah. Every time I would go to my aunt's house, she would give me capfuls of Peach Schnapps to put me to sleep, and I remember that, and I remember wanting to go to her house just for that.

Kimber Lynne: Really?

Chayne: Yes, ma'am.

Kimber Lynne: Wow! So, as a 3-year-old, you already were experiencing a taste that you wanted and a feeling of peaceful, calmness because of that?

Chayne: I guess. Yeah. I just knew that I liked it.

Kimber Lynne: Okay. So, when you're ten years old, what's happening?

Chayne: I had tried marijuana when I was eight years old.

Kimber Lynne: Who gave you marijuana at eight?

Chayne: My mother's second husband. We were going to get fitted for tuxedos for their wedding and he had a bong in his car. He would hit his bong and he would let me clear the smoke out of it.

Kimber Lynne: What did you think of that as an eight-year-old?

Chayne: Really, I grew up around marijuana my whole life, so I didn't think anything of it. I just knew that when people smoked it, they were happy and they had fun, and so.

Kimber Lynne: So, was your mother a user?

Chayne: Yeah. She smoked marijuana frequently around me. I was just told not to talk about it at school because it would get her in trouble.

Kimber Lynne: So, you didn't talk about it at school?

Chayne: No, ma'am. No, ma'am.

Kimber Lynne: Yeah. Not talking about that. Were you an only child?

Chayne: I've got an older brother, but he grew up with my grandparents, so-

Kimber Lynne: So, basically-

Chayne: Basically, I grew up as an only child. Yes, ma'am.

Kimber Lynne: Any other drugs going on in the house that you knew of at the time?

Chayne: There was drinking, marijuana, but I know there was cocaine use, but I didn't know it at the time.

Kimber Lynne: You never witnessed it, or didn't know what cocaine was?

Chayne: No. If it was done in front of me, I don't remember it or, but I had heard about it. But I didn't really know, just really from what I heard in school.

Kimber Lynne: So, "Pot" or "Weed" in the scheme of this conversation about opioids is not really a big deal except that we believe it is a gateway drug to more dangerous substances.

Chayne: No. Yeah.

Kimber Lynne: It's when we start getting to the all-star drugs that totally take you out of life.

Chayne: Yes, ma'am.

Kimber Lynne: Which drug is that for you?

Chayne: That's probably cocaine and heroin.

Kimber Lynne: Tell me when that happened and how that took you out of the game.

Chayne: Well, my first struggle with cocaine, I first used when I was 14 years old. I used everything when I was 14, tried it all, but I became pretty much an everyday cocaine user at the age of 19, 20.

Kimber Lynne: How were you getting it?

Chayne: I had a good job. I would work all week and then come Friday I would blow my money, blow it all, and usually by the next Monday I was broke. That went on until I was about 24. I hadn't used heroin yet. I hadn't really used pills yet either, but I spiraled out of control pretty bad by the time I was 24. I was smoking crack and doing cocaine, and I had started injecting it by then.

Kimber Lynne: Did that scare you? When you first said, "I hear people doing this. It's a faster high. It lasts longer." Is that why you crossed that line? Were you scared?

Chayne: No. I wasn't scared. I just wanted to get the full benefit. If I was going to spend $20 on it, I wanted all $20 of it in my bloodstream, kind of. And my friends were doing it, so that took the fear out of it, watching them try it and they were fine, so…

Kimber Lynne: So, it's kind of an oxymoron for me. I hear these stories and hear the word "friend." They can't be good "friends" if they're allowing you to do this to yourself.

Chayne: Nah, but they were sick just like I was and we were in it together, kind of, and a lot of them are still sick out there now. They just haven't got to where I'm trying to get to myself. It got out of control, and I got sent to rehab when I was 24.

Kimber Lynne: You got sent there? It wasn't by choice?

Chayne: Yeah, court ordered.

Kimber Lynne: Court ordered. Okay.

Chayne: Yes, ma'am.

Kimber Lynne: So, here's the deal. Based on what I've learned in the last two years, court order makes you go. You go because you don't want jail time. "Okay, I'll go." Don't want to go. Don't really want to stop what I'm doing because I'm really; I'm okay with what I'm doing." So, you go because it's court-ordered, but it doesn't fix you until you decide, "I need it for me."

Chayne: Yes. Yes, ma'am. It was good in the sense that I got educated on my disease, and I learned the root of it. I learned that using drugs was just a symptom of a deeper problem, which actually was my thinking, and I found out that, that's what I needed to correct. I wasn't ready to do that yet. I got out, and I continued to use for ten more years, but at least by going there, I found out where I could go to get help when I was ready.

▲ ▲ ▲

At this point, you may be saying that your kid is nothing like Chayne, maybe you can relate to Diane's or Jill's story as to how they first were introduced to a drug of choice. Like I said previously, all the stories marry each other in some way or another. My kids were accepted by their peers, outgoing for the most part, and gifted in several ways – of course, they are all of that I'm their mother telling the story. In reality, parents don't often see issues of low self-esteem or struggles in the social aspects of high school or the peer pressures that occur in relationships. Marie's transcript speaks volumes about every aspect of a world filled with anxiety, pressures, acceptance, and self-worth.

Kimber Lynne: When do you remember the very first time you took an opiate?

Marie: It was actually my father's medication. This was probably my senior year in high school, and he had been prescribed medication for a couple of years, and it was left on his counter and I just remember thinking, "I wonder if that would be fun to take?" And I did. I took about eight pills from his bottle, and I took them to school with me and I used them during school.

Kimber Lynne: Had you tried pot?

Marie: Sure. I was a senior in high school at that time. I was dating a guy who was in a grade above me, and he offered me to come to this party.

I remember they were all smoking pot, and they asked me if I'd like to try it. I said yes, and we were smoking out of this huge bong, and I didn't know how to do it, and they had to show me how to do it. And I remember just sitting there the whole time out of my mind quiet, shy, paranoid, but for some reason, I liked the way it felt.

Kimber Lynne: There's always those kids that are in the popular group, and they're going to kind of follow and be cool. There are people that say, "I don't really care about being cool, but I want to try that," and then there will be the one that says, "I'm not gonna do anything to disappoint my parents." Which kid were you?

Marie: I was the kid in the popular group who wanted to please everybody. I was a people pleaser, and if they were doing it more than likely, I was going to try it. It was the things that I was bottling down inside, the numbing, the lack of relationship with my father. The always not feeling I fit in with my peers and always feeling I had to somehow act differently, and the only way I could act differently and act more like them was with putting a drug inside of me.

Kimber Lynne: Dabbling is one thing, but when did it become more than what you could handle?

Marie: I was in a state of depression, situational depression to where I couldn't get this great job, so I came home and was working at a salon.

Kimber Lynne

The day that was my weakest moment was the day that somebody offered me painkillers when I was in that state of depression. I knew exactly what it was, and of course, I took it a week later. This person came back in with basically a bag full about fifty to a hundred pills and just gave them to me for no cost. It was probably six months into that relationship, you know, friendship relationship him coming into the salon that he saw what was going on because I would ask him for them every time he came in and he decided to stop.

So here, I'm fully addicted to painkillers, and my means of getting them have stopped. So, I had to go to the streets to get them.

3

INSIDE DAILY STRUGGLES OF ADDICTION

▲ ▲ ▲

"I woke up in some sort of campground with two strangers and I had been using the whole night. When I woke up, I realized I was in the middle of nowhere. My cellphone was dead. I had no car, no ride and I was stranded in the woods with two strangers."

▲ ▲ ▲

Simply stated, I feel as though I have a parental degree in drug addiction. I can't tell you how many parents I have spoken to that have become passionate about this disease. Even more so, these same parents have expressed that they too could write a book about their experience! When you are playing an investigative reporter in your own home trying to make sense of what is going on, you literally drive yourself crazy.

Your child is telling you one thing and you can't come to the conclusion that what they are telling you is the truth. The stories never quite add up. And you can never prove what you know. What you don't know is the constant struggle your child is going through trying to cover up their addiction and hoping to get clean without anyone knowing. Jill's story is heart-breaking as she tries desperately to get free of her addiction.

Kimber Lynne: So, the more you take, the more you need to feel normal, which people don't understand.

Jill: Right.

Kimber Lynne: If they don't understand addiction, where they're like, "What do you mean feel normal? You're just trying to get high."

Jill: Right.

Kimber Lynne: Set them straight?

Jill: Okay. That's tough. If you don't use, you don't live. I mean the way that your mind tells you, I mean the physical sickness is a real thing, I mean from opiates. When you aren't taking it, you're actually physically sick. I guess they say that you can't die from coming off of detoxing from opiates, but it feels like dying. It's not even quite getting normal when you're using; it's really, you would call it getting straight.

When I woke up in the morning, if I woke up in the morning, sometimes I never went to sleep. But when I woke up, it was the first thing that I thought about. It wasn't breathing; it wasn't showering; it wasn't brushing your teeth. It was, I didn't have enough money to get the next one. Or, if I do, where am I gonna get it? How am I gonna get it? And it didn't stop until Groundhog Day. Until the next day, when it was the same exact thing, over, and over, and over.

Once you are taking it regularly, there's no way to just stop. I think that's another misconception that people have that you can just stop. You can't. You need help to stop. I tried to stop so many times, and I could. I consider myself to be pretty tough, so I could stop using when I realized that things were getting really hard for me. And I kept having these flashes of reality. Like, you can't keep doing this.

I would stop for a period of time. I would stop for three days. I would go through that pain. The cold sweats and that feeling like you're dying. I would go through that. I would put myself through that. I would say, "Look, I'm not addicted. I can do this. This is fine." But where would I be a week later? I'd be right back in it. So it was that constant cycle of I'm gonna stop, I'm gonna stop. I'm gonna stay stopped, but I could never stay stopped, not until I got help.

Kimber Lynne: Darkest day?

Jill: The darkest day. The first thing that comes to mind is, I had to do certain things to get money. All of these I'd swear, that any woman would swear they would never do. I woke up in some sort of campground with two strangers, and I had been using the whole night. When I woke up, I realized I was in the middle of nowhere. My cellphone was dead. I had no car, no ride, and I was stranded in the woods with two strangers.

Eventually, one of them had a ride. There was no vehicle there. I mean I don't know how we got there, but I woke up in a tent, and there was no vehicle there. So how am I gonna get back to my house? I need to feed my cat. So eventually, one of the men that were there got someone to come give them a ride, so they could get out and go do whatever they want to do. It's very hazy. I was also still using the next day.

But I was able to get a ride from the campground to the man's house, which was in the town; but still several, several miles away from where I was staying at the time. So, I begged them, like, "Please, just drop me off at my place." Like, "No. All you're gonna get is a ride to where we're going." I had flip-flops on. My phone was dead. I couldn't call anyone for a ride. It was hot, and I had to walk. I started walking. I mean, what else was I gonna do? I started walking to my apartment, and the concrete was hot on my feet. It was burning my feet, but I couldn't walk in the grass because there were sand spurs in the grass.

I don't know how long it would've taken me to get home, but someone drove past me really slow. I'm like, who is this gonna be? Like, some guy's gonna whistle at me, or whatever. They came back around, and it was actually someone else that I knew that I was selling my body to. At that point, I realized, I'm a well-known town prostitute. This man, I'm in the middle of nowhere walking to where I live, and someone completely separate from the stuff that I had gotten into that night, recognized me. "Oh, let me give you a ride back to your place." I'm like, "What are the odds?" Well, apparently, the odds are really high. Apparently, I really get around.

That's not anything I would ever plan to be proud of. So, I got a ride with him, and he gave me money and told me to call him. And I got back to my place. That was definitely one of the last times that I remember. When you get clean, they tell you, "Remember your last run because it'll keep you from thinking that it'll be a good idea to use again."

That's what comes to mind, is walking on the side of the road. My flip-flops were giving me blisters, so it was more comfortable to have the concrete burn my feet. And then this other man, it was so degrading. And to think that you could correlate those little blue pills putting me in a place like that. It's like a movie. It's like a story. You wouldn't even believe it unless you've lived it, I guess.

Kimber Lynne: Did you ever cross to heroin?

Jill: I did not use heroin. Well, I did not shoot heroin. I probably used heroin more times than I even know of, because I would use whatever was in front of me. However, when I was using Percocet, the highest milligram, they're very expensive. On the street, they go for $30 if you don't know someone. So, a $30 high with a Percocet is a $5 high with heroin and it'll last longer. I knew that, but I was doing everything I could, like, I would be okay as long as I didn't start using heroin. Then I'm not an addict. Then I don't have a problem. Then I can still manage this.

▲ ▲ ▲

The scariest part about interviewing recovering addicts is that I know deep down inside their stories are similar to the life my child was living. If you are a parent reading this and trying to understand, it's going to be difficult for you too. Oh, but for the Grace of God. I believe. You will never get these details from a loved one and I suppose it is a blessing. But if you are to truly understand and help your child, neighbor, or significant other, it might be beneficial to hear. Only you can be the judge of that. To me, hearing these stories correlates to gambling. You start off spending a little and then it escalates to where there will never be enough money to stay ahead. Diane outlines the progression of just that. Prescription opioids skyrocketing to where she had to do what she never thought she would.

Diane: So, like, I said, I had 20 bucks, and I was sick. I was like, "Screw it. I'm going to close my eyes. You do it for me." You know, I just didn't want to feel bad. So, I let him shoot me up, and I'll never forget it because it was the most amazing, but sickening feeling I had ever had. It went from the top of my head to the end of my toes and it was literally the best feeling I have ever felt in my entire life. And at that moment, I knew that I was screwed. I knew that it had me, and I didn't care. I didn't care.

My thought was, why did I wait so long? Why did I wait so long? Why did I waste all that money? But, just as in the very beginning, I had no idea what I was about to go through.

Once I crossed that barrier, you know, I was right. I became a super addict. The withdrawals were intensified by a thousand. It would start at five o'clock in the morning, every morning. I would wake up, and I would yawn, and from that very first yawn, I would feel the nausea. And I was throwing up every morning at five in the morning.

And that's just enough to make you angry. I mean mad, cause first off, I don't like mornings. Never have. You know, if it was up to me I would sleep until one o'clock every day. You know, I think that came with the sickness and the depression. So, the fact that I was waking up and seeing the number five, I was just furious, and I was sick as a dog on top of it. So, at five in the morning was when I started my fucked-up day.

Who am I going to rob? Probably my family. When I first started, you know, the whole shooting up thing I was like, I'm not going to get addicted to this. I knew it had me, but I was like I don't know how to do it myself, so I'll be okay. I can't have track marks cause my family will see it. I'll be okay. You know, this isn't something that I can do every day. That's what I told myself. I stopped caring. I think I snorted it one more time and was like never again.

Never again. It just did not compare. So, I tried it myself one day, and eventually, I thought I could go to school for phlebotomy cause I was damn good at it. I could hit anyone, anywhere. It didn't matter. I got good at it and I was screwed. I went from this, like, innocent kid that would never do drugs to this full-blown junkie that was stealing from my family that loved me the most and not caring if I lived or died.

And, now that I think back on it, it's almost like it wasn't my life. I still can't believe that that was me. I still can't believe that I did the things that I did.

Kimber Lynne: Did you ever OD?

Diane: Yeah. Honestly, I got really lucky for a really long time. I had friends of mine that OD'd. I brought two of my friends back to life. One was really bad because I shot him up. We got the dope together and I shot him up and he went into the living room and I was fixing mine and he was already messed up. He was talking and mumbling. I couldn't understand what he was saying; he was running into walls. He had been up for a couple days. He was on Ambien. You know, he was on a concoction of things.

And I was like, you know, just sit down. Sit down on the couch, wait 'til I come in there. You know, just chill out. Let me do my thing. So, he sits down and I'm in the kitchen and I didn't hear him anymore. And I was like, "Hey! Hey, what's up. Hey!" No response. So, I go in there, and he's purple, and I mean purple. I have never, ever, you know, I haven't seen a dead body. I've never experienced anything like that, nearly like that. You know, I saw one person have a seizure one time and it about traumatized me.

So, this was way, way out of my norm. So, anyway, he's blue. Purplish, blue and I'm slapping him and I'm throwing water on him and nothing was working. I was trying to give him mouth to mouth. He was doing what's called the "death rattle," which is the gurgling type, snoring-ish noise. And basically, what it means is his lungs are filling up with fluid. So, I knew that I had to do something. So, I called the cops and the EMT and they had to hit him with a Narcan shot three times to bring him back.

And the whole time I'm waiting for them to get here, you know, you'd think that since it just almost killed my buddy,

I'd get rid of the drugs. You know, flush them or something. No, I was trying to do all the drugs. Like, my drugs and his drugs. I'm trying to do all the drugs, and I did. I did all the drugs. It was crazy. You know, I just about killed him and I just chalked it up to he was on a bunch of drugs. He was on Ambien and that did it. He woke up in the hospital and thanked me for saving his life and asked me where the drugs were.

And I told him that I had done them and that they were gone. And when he got out, we went and got some more from the same guy; didn't die that time though. My experience with overdosing is, I don't know, I just kind of chalk it up to my life. You know, this would happen to me, kind of thing. I just feel like my karma is horrible, but I was down in the dumps. I was at my bottom and I was waiting for a month and a half to get on the methadone program in my town.

And it was January 31st that I was supposed to start dosing, and on January 30th, I was with a friend of mine and I had 60 dollars. I had gotten 40 dollars worth of heroin and I shot it up and I was fine. I had 20 dollars left that I was going to save for the next morning and a random friend of mine, somebody that I hadn't seen in a long time called me and was like, "Hey, got some really good shit. You need to try it." The one guy that I gave it to, he got a 20 and about passed out kind of thing.

He basically was like if you don't get a buzz off of it, I'll give you your money back. Hey, drug dealer with money-back guarantee? I'm all over that. It sounded great. I mean, yeah count me in. So, that's exactly what I did. I was all over it. I went right over there, and I was like, "Look, all I got is 20 bucks." He's like, "That's fine. That's all you need." So, I was like okay, sure let's do it. So, we go get it, and I was driving my dad's car and we got the drugs and we went to a gas station in town where I shot up because I was ... As soon as you get your drugs you don't wait 'til you go to your house.

You know what I mean? You just don't. You do it anywhere and everywhere. So, the last thing I remember is doing my shot in that parking lot. And I woke up about; I think it was 45 minutes later. So, that's 45 minutes that I can't account for, but I was in a different place. I was no longer at the gas station. My car had been driven up the road to the Burger King, which was like two miles up the road. So, I went from somehow in the driver's seat; I don't know if he jumped on top of me and drove the truck there. I don't know if he picked me up and moved me out and then put me back.

Cause I woke up back in the driver's seat, but basically whatever happened, I was in this new parking lot by myself and basically, he got scared and thought that I was dead. So, instead of calling an ambulance or just dropping me off at the hospital, he just left. He just ran and I don't know. I guess he didn't want to get in trouble. So, good friend, you know. I'd known this kid since kindergarten. Okay, like, one of them I could trust, you know. So, you know I'd like to think that I wasn't raped or anything like that. I don't know.

I don't know why I woke up at all. Nobody woke me up. He did tell me that when he left me, I was blue and not breathing. So, I don't know why I'm here. I don't know; I guess because there's a purpose for my life. That's kind of like, what I like to think. But that was my most intense, scariest overdose. The day before I was supposed to start dosing and fix my life, you know. I almost died. Yes, so that was pretty awesome. Not.

Kimber Lynne: Wow.

▲ ▲ ▲

In the two years I spent interviewing about the opioid crisis, I spoke with a couple of individuals whose addiction was the result of a medical procedure or treatment. You think a few pain pills after a procedure couldn't possibly get you addicted. You might want to rethink this. It is a scary fact and a realization that makes you thirsty for a different way to control pain, not just for your child but for yourself as well. Michelle was uprooted from her life in New York in middle school. The first friends she met were potheads, so she says. She had said no to smoking marijuana numerous times with her new friends, but after a while, she then decided it was no big deal, and she tried it.

A few years had passed, where she started to experience some neck and back pain and was prescribed pain medication. When the pain seemed a little more severe, she would increase her dosage until she was running out of her prescription weeks before the next script was to be filled.

Michelle, like the others, was forced to leave the security and safety of the Pharma world and went to the streets to ratify her addiction.

Kimber Lynne: Did it ever get to a point where you had to go to the street?

Michelle: Yes.

Kimber Lynne: Did you ever cross the line? Did you go to heroin?

Michelle: Yes.

Kimber Lynne: Do you remember the first time and what you were feeling and whether you were scared? Do you remember how it was administered, and what you thought of the future? Did you even care at that point?

Michelle: Let's see. I snorted it. That was the way that I did the drugs or did the opiates at that point and I was only snorting them well, like when I would run out of my medication. I would then, you know, whatever money I had, I would just try to find some more pills of course at the best deal that I could and then, of course, someone that we knew and trusted would start telling us that they were using heroin. Me and my boyfriend were like that's disgusting what's wrong with you? And we would talk maybe a week about how gross that was and the next thing, you know, we were hanging out with them one day. That's what your addiction does, it tells you it's okay to be around these people that are doing this crap. And so of course, somebody always offers it to you. I mean, in my opinion, everyone that I've ever known that is on heroin now all got started from prescription pain medicine.

Kimber Lynne: Some of the stuff is so strong that when the First Responders get on scene, they can actually die from being exposed to what is being sold. Does that ever enter an addict's mind that "I'm not sure I want to move to that, kind of thing?"

Michelle: Somebody had a pill printing machine, and they were printing off fentanyl pills and pretending they were Percocet 30's. Like it's just all the stuff that just started one after one, just causing me to feel more fear and anxiety about it. And then one day the boyfriend I was with, he overdosed in front of me. I didn't know exactly what was going on until, you know, I couldn't wake him up. He was hunched over on the chair. And to make matters worse, we were at my mother's apartment. I would have bet a million dollars that he was dead. His skin was gray, and his lips were blue, and I couldn't wake him up and I was shaking him, trying to wake him up. I ended up having to grab him by the shirt to drag him into the bathroom, where I was going to put him in the shower. That's all I knew. I also knew that if the brain doesn't get oxygen for four minutes, then he would be brain dead. So, I already had in my mind that calling the ambulance isn't even going to help because he's literally, like I already thought, he was dead. For some reason, I had grabbed a cold bottle of water. I'm sitting in the bathroom, and I'm trying to lift him up to put him in the tub. And I'm hysterically crying and I'm like shaking him and somehow, I guess by the Grace of God this bottle of water spilled on his, on his foot and the cold hitting his extremities I guess shocked him back. The color went back in his skin, and he looked up at me while I'm crying hysterically and I have my head hung down cause I can't even look at him at this point and he's like, "What's wrong babe?"

Kimber Lynne

Kimber Lynne: Did you use again, after that?

Michelle: Of course. I used again after that. Yes, but I always used the smallest amount possible to not be sick because that was literally the only thing that I was concerned with at that point. I didn't have a prescription to Suboxone at the time and I did not want to go to the Methadone program because when I was in active addiction I would take methadone to get high and I mean that's what it does, it gets people high, you know, so I didn't want anything to do with that.

What I learned in the drug-dealing world is that it's hard to stop. You can find it on any street corner in any town at any time. Are you in control of your child's phone? By that, I mean, are you paying the bills? Take a look at the text stream if you are. You can't actually see what is being typed, but you can see how many minutes are used and how much text data is being used. I was able to get phone numbers and saw a pattern. I plugged some of the phone numbers into Facebook, and a couple of times, the dealer's page was revealed and I knew that the picture I was seeing on social media wasn't the circle of friends that my child had grown up around. It wasn't so much the physical appearance of the person, it was the language and subject matter on their page. It was obvious that it was merely a transactional acquaintance. A provider of drugs. It was at this time I knew that my suspicions were correct and that there was indeed a problem. With that knowledge, I was armed with questions for this interview with Wayne.

Kimber Lynne: Is it true when you hear parents say, watch who your kids are hanging out with because that's where it all starts?

Wayne: That's true. Absolutely. Absolutely.

Kimber Lynne: Could it have been stopped? Early on? Could your parents have identified who you were hanging out with, and would you have taken a different road?

Wayne: You know, that's hard to say really, um, I think at such an early age you just want to be accepted. You want to fit in. I think that's how it really started. When I first tried alcohol, I hated it. I hated the taste of it, you know, it was disgusting. But that's what my friends were doing, so I just did what I did so I could fit in. I was in AG classes as a child. I went to church every Sunday. I had a very good upbringing and I think my parents were just trying to block it out of their mind until I could get it under control. They were thinking my son doesn't really have a problem, you know, he's just experimenting. He will grow out of it – Things of that nature.

Kimber Lynne: I'm seeing the picture of an honor roll student, goes to church with the family. When was it not playing around – experimenting and when was it an actual addiction?

Wayne: I would say around when I first started to experiment with cocaine. So probably around 18-19 years old. I got in a relationship and had a child at a very young age. I was 18. Coming from a religious background, my parents kind of pushed me into, you know, telling me I needed to marry her, so to speak. So, we did that and we were just so young and the marriage was just so rocky. I believe that's when I realized I had an addiction. When I was going

Kimber Lynne

through the separation and divorce at such a young age, I think that's when my addiction really took over. I was just depressed and felt like I had let my family down. My parents have been married for 40 years, you know, and that was hard. I am 19-20 years old and already going through a separation. That's when the drinking and the cocaine really got out of control.

Kimber Lynne: The addiction had become bad enough that you had to turn to selling to support your habit? What was the worst "drug" day where you could have lost your life?

Wayne: My girlfriend was pregnant at the time, and our house was invaded by four people in the middle of the night and we were tied up pistol-whipped and robbed. But even that wasn't my breaking point. For the first time, I just lived in so much fear.

Kimber Lynne: I would like to ask the next series of questions because it's hard to comprehend someone selling a drug that they are not certain whether or not it's pure. Is it fair to say that the dealer doesn't care if someone dies, they don't care who they sell to? Dealers don't really know the quality of what they are selling because it is coming off the streets. Did you care what you were selling? Did you know whether it was good stuff, bad stuff, laced with fentanyl, cut with X-Y-Z?

Wayne: You know, really, I didn't. I would try to justify things because I did have morals instilled in me as a kid. I knew right from wrong. I would justify it by maybe paying somebody's light bill, or if I saw a homeless person, I'd give him a new pair of shoes. It was just self-justification. I was told a lot of times the heroin that I was selling was not cut with fentanyl, but I mean, there's no way that they could have determined that really. I was a drug dealer and also an addict, so I was willing to do whatever it took. Of course, I didn't want to harm people. I really didn't.

Kimber Lynne: Did you ever hear of anybody overdosing on something you sold them?

Wayne: No. Luckily. I never heard of anybody. Most of the drugs I sold were cocaine crack. It was towards the very end that I got involved selling heroin. Like, I said, my source would tell me that it wasn't cut with fentanyl. But there was no way of him really knowing that. We're taking the chance for certain, you know, we could have very possibly killed somebody and looking back, I mean maybe I didn't sell something directly to somebody who OD'd, but I could have got them started down that path that led them to overdose.

4

WHEN IT GETS TO THE POINT LOCK THEM UP TO SAVE THEM

▲▲▲

"Best thing for her to do is be arrested because she's just on this self-destruction course and has to be arrested."

▲▲▲

Timothy: I had to tell my wife. I was like, "She's doing drugs". And the hurtful look on my wife's face, I was afraid that she would be mad at me for how Ebony was. My wife, of course, she was like, I've been through this with you, I can't deal with this. She had a meltdown and we were going to send Ebony to treatment at 16. She had about three more months to go in school, I was like, well, I don't want to pull her out of school she'll get left back a year. This, that and the other. I was just bearing all the guilt of it. It was all me; this is all my fault. She was doing this, but it was all my fault, all my making.

And I decided not to send her to treatment because they wouldn't keep her school curriculum up, it'd be pulling her out of band and band was going to get her a scholarship. I decided not to do it. Because I was in recovery now, I took her to NA. I remember the good people in NA told me, you know Tim, you can bring a horse to water, but you can't make them drink. The same thing applied to her as anybody else. Recovery is not for people who need it. It's for people who want it.

And she didn't want it. She did it because her dad brought her, made her. That's when I knew I was dealing with a full-blown addict replica of myself.

Kimber Lynne: How long did this go on for?

Timothy: What, the...

Kimber Lynne: The whole addiction?

Timothy: Well, there was ebbs and flows, you know, I told her when she started to get towards 18, I was like, you know, you don't have to have the life I had with this addiction. You don't have to. Keep it together, man, because you're smarter than me. You're better than me. You can beat this thing and she started doing good. She was doing good in high school. In high school, she made all-district band. I think her senior year when she was in band; her high school football team won the state championship. She had become the band major in high school, direct the whole high school marching band. She made that. She was just, she directed, we were going to church, she directed the church choir sometimes. She just had, musically, she was just talented, and she had the brains.

There were some people from colleges that wanted her. They come when the band would perform in high school, they'd come see her. They were like, yeah, we'll give her a scholarship. I was like, wow and I was thinking maybe the nightmare, that legacy of mine, is not coming true. Maybe it's not coming true; maybe, she can live her way out of this. We managed to get her sent off to college. I was so glad, I was like, phew. She's not another me. I think she was still messing around but she wasn't doing hard drugs, as far as I know, just smoking weed and stuff. I say, oh, college kids, you know. She's not a full-blown chemical addict like me.

That came crashing down. We sent her to college; she was smart, I was like, you could go to college and for extra money, you know, work a little side job, extra money. What your grants don't cover you have the extra spending money. Ebony's thinking was, how about if I get you to sign for a loan, this was her thinking, she got a supplemental loan with my signature. Got money, bought a package of dope, do some, sell some. Why work a regular job like anybody else? And that's what she had going on in college.

Until she sold to an undercover officer, I get a phone call, well my wife got a phone call. My wife comes to me one day after work. I'm like, something's off. She's like, "Ebony's in jail." I'm like, what happened? Why? Only thing in my mind, she's an addict like you. I'm like, what in the world. She came to give me a story of, we were getting high and the cops pulled us and she gave me some lying story. What happened was she sold weed to an undercover cop.

So they kicked her out of college. Some friends from college signed her out of jail after a weekend or something and I had to go there and get her. I was like, what do you have to finish in school? She goes, well I have trigonometry exams to finish. Trigonometry, that's how smart she was. I was like, okay. So, she went and took her exams. Still kicked out but finished it. And she passed the exams and I'm like trigonometry and she's, addicts are smart people.

Anyway, she got sent home, back to my house. On house arrest, and that's when the nightmare, the heavy stuff, came in. It really got bad, the lying, the weed, the pills, the bad people. Friends like herself, you know, high school buddies that got high with you, they were still there in town. The ones who were off to college were off. It started; she just started getting heavier and heavier.

Until, one day, I figured she was doing something heavy. I didn't know what it was. I didn't think it was heroin. She was doing something heavy because of the way she would act. One day I was at work, and at this point, I had told my wife, you know, she can't drive our vehicles because she's getting high. I can't have her driving our vehicles. She's going to kill somebody, kill herself. I was trying to do everything I could to fix her, me and my wife, both. We couldn't fix her. I think, at that point, we were enabling her, trying to fix her. We're just enabling her to keep doing what she's doing, with our best intentions.

Kimber Lynne

One day I came home from work, and my wife had a look on her face. My daughter was sitting there. I'm like, okay. I pull up my driveway and the trailblazer I just bought, you know, paid off after six years of payments, wasn't in the driveway. I'm like, maybe Janet's out shopping or something. I go in the house; my wife's there, my daughter's there. I'm like; you're here, the trailblazers not here, I'm like, where's the trailblazer? My wife gave me a look like, I'm like, oh God, this is not good. She's like, Ebony was in an accident. And then, of course, my minds like, was somebody hurt, did somebody get killed, the insurance company, somebody's going to sue me, we're going down.

My temperature started to rise. I'm like, this whole thing is a B.S. lie. She was and I could tell, looking at her at the house, she was high then. She wasn't where she was supposed to be, wasn't supposed to be driving and wrecked my damn brand new vehicle. I came back. I was hot. I was hot. So, I come back home from that, my wife went somewhere and Ebony was gone. I was like, you know, I can't anymore. She started to tear our lives down. I went into her room; I'm gonna invade her privacy, yeah, addicts they have no privacy in your home. I went in her room, scrounged around, I saw a box. A box about yay big when you get from the pharmacist when you buy hypodermic needles you get a box of them, and she hadn't hidden it. They get a little sloppy.

It all became clear. She's scoring dope for her friends, getting a good chunk, giving them theirs, bagging up the rest of it, and selling it. Out of my house! Selling heroin out of my house, I mean without a doubt.

I saw her when she just happened to be coming from the dope direction (the place where she was buying drugs) and I call the police, you know, I was so upset. I wanted to get her out, but I went to the police and they said you gotta wait 90 days to get them out of your house. I was like, I'm calling the police I'm going to show them this. Best thing for her to do is be arrested because she's just on this self-destruction course and has to be arrested. I can't do anything, you know. So, I call the cops and he came, she came back to the yard from the dope direction and he tried the cop thing like you know this stuff will ruin your life and she's like, uh-huh. I was like, what I need is her to leave the premise. She can't stay here, no more.

I was angry, and my heart was breaking at the same time. I said we can't do this here anymore. Do with her what you need to, but she just can't stay here. And he looks at her like okay, you know that you have to leave the premise. I said she can go in and get whatever she needs clothes. She goes, I'm fine. I was like, okay. I think she took like a little bag or something. I thought he was going to arrest her, take her downtown. Shocked me, he gave her the box back.

Kimber Lynne: What?

Timothy: And he said, you have somewhere to go? And she happened to have some friends around the corner, wanting to take her wherever. She goes, I have some friends. She probably knew I was going to kick her out, but the cop gave her the box back. She walked off and I looked at him, like, I'm thinking, did that just happen? He goes, there's nothing we could do. She hasn't actually committed a crime. I was like, "She possesses paraphernalia". He goes, it was something like, we can't do anything at this point. Something he said and I was in such dumbfounded awe I was like, I can't believe it.

So, after that, we got some peace in the house. Stuff stopped missing. Before you could lay your wallet, your backpack around, jewelry going missing. My daughter had a big screen TV in the house. One day I came home and she was walking to a car with the big screen TV putting it in the car. I said, what are you doing? This is my TV dad, I need this or I'm not going to have a place to stay tonight. I was like, go ahead and take your TV. Let me check my house. What happened, she got a ladder from inside the shed, went through a bedroom window, broke into the house. I was like, you know I could call the police on her, but I'm not gonna do it. She's got her TV, if she comes back on these premises, then I will.

Of course, my wife came home, and the big screen TV was gone and she had a melt-down, again. I was like, yeah, Ebony came and took it. Fortunately, at this time, I'm in recovery, and things are well for me. I had money in the bank, went and bought another big-screen TV. Momma happy. I said, our girl has just gone off the rails, bad. She comes up here again, I'm pressing charges. We love her but, now she's starting to victimize us. Every time you leave, she's gonna come in and rob the house. That was that.

After that, it was just a series of we didn't hear from her weeks, months, at a time. And somebody in the family, be like, yeah Ebony's in jail. Because her picture would be in the paper.

Kimber Lynne: **Right.**

Timothy: **I'm like, okay. Just living with, kinda, the shame of that.**

▲ ▲ ▲

Once you realize that your child is in the throes of full addiction, you think that you have some control to fix it; to stop it. Somewhere in the back of your mind, you believe you can sit down and have a rational conversation about getting them help and are naive enough to think they will listen. You spend countless sleepless nights worrying. You strategize about catching them in the act to get the proof you need to make them go to rehab. Alan was very proactive in his quest to help his daughter.

Alan: **She was on our cell phone plan. And the only thing we could actually get off of it was the numbers, and so we would call all them. And of course, it didn't take much to figure out who you were talking to if they answered the phone. We would turn those telephone numbers over to the police department, and they would check them and said, "Yes, you're right. They are drug dealers that we are actively watching at this time." My daughter, her car was in my name, my insurance was on it.**

So that's one of the first things I did. She was over 21. I took her off of my insurance for fear that she was going to kill

somebody, and then it would come back to me. I mean, I followed her as much as I could. She left one time and went to go get drugs and met a drug dealer in our little store here. And I came up behind her and drove a truck up behind her and blocked her in so she couldn't get out. And called the Sheriff's department, and she backed up and hit my truck. Didn't hit it hard, and I said, "You give it your best."

I said, "Because I'm not leaving." And I thought a deputy would show up, but I ended up getting six deputies and the rescue squad at a store, and then it's like, "Oh my God, what have I done?" "Look at me." I was fortunate enough that if you work with a lot of these officers that they know you and they know what you're going through. Their mindset has now changed from let's put this sorry son of a gun into jail to actually get them help.

So, the officer looked at me, and I told him what was going on. I said, "She's going to drive out. She's going to be driving out of here under the influence and die or kill somebody." And he looked at my truck, and it was just painted. He said, "Did she hit your truck?" I said, "Yes, sir." He said, "Were you in it?" I realized real quick; it was just this versus a felony. So, I said, "No, I was not." He said, "Do you want me to hold her here until you go get a warrant on her?" I said, Yes, sir, I do."

So, I drove, went and got a warrant on her, and they threw her in jail for the second time. So, we did that. And I think, all in all, she went to jail three times, and the last time through the court system we got her held there until she could get what was called bed ready and help. But I just feared that she was going to run into somebody and kill them, you know? So, I just wanted her off the street.

Kimber Lynne: During the time she was in jail, was there peace of mind?

Alan: Yes, I knew where she was. I know she's not doing drugs. Her attorney said, "If you've got any connections in the jail system, she needs this – this and this- that she won't have." (referring to withdraw symptoms and getting help detoxing with Suboxone, Methadone or some other prescription substance). So, I went to the sheriff, and I said, "My lawyer said I needed this, this, and this." And he said, "Come with me." We went back in the nurse's station. They checked everything and got it and carried it back to her. Law enforcement at that time, this was 2016 going into 2017, they were getting a better attitude, and so was the district attorney about the disease of addiction.

We got on a first name basis, trying to get help for people like my daughter. These were not criminals. He told me, he said, "Now if you're dealing," he said, "I'm going to put you under the jail." He said, "But going through my court system," he said, "We're not going to put you in jail. It's set to hold you there until we can get you help." He said, "These are not mean people." He said, "They've been caught up with this disease." I don't know about the term disease or whatever you want to call it, but that whole mindset had changed by the people in law enforcement and the court system because I think it started hitting lawyers and doctors and middle-class people, upper-middle-class people, and so forth. So, their attitudes changed after that.

Kimber Lynne

Kimber Lynne: Was she ready at that time? Was she crying out, saying, "I'm ready, I want help?"

Alan: Absolutely not. They sent her to Blue Ridge in the end of North Carolina and the first 30 days, she couldn't have any calls or any contact. What she was in was a worldwide program with Celebrate Recovery. That's when she came and told me that I needed to go see them. So, we did.

They gave us a lot of good pointers about the enabling. But the stupidest thing that rehab place did after 30 days was allow their clients to choose any individual, they wanted to come visit. The individual my daughter chose was her boyfriend, that was on drugs too. He carried her drugs and a cell phone and got her kicked out. And I'm thinking and you are running a rehab? How stupid can you be? But the vast majority of them (rehab facilities) through our research, don't have a very high success rate for clients going through for the first time. A lot of times, you're going back three times and sometimes three times doesn't work. And until either you decide that you want to stop or either you're dead, that's your two choices.

Kimber Lynne: When did she decide? How long did it take, or did she not ever decide she just stayed long enough to stay clean?

Alan: I think the most help she got was when she found somebody that had been where she was and they had been successful in recovery and she accepted them as a mentor.

So, all you can do is educate yourself. And if that parent doesn't educate their self and are not willing to do all the bad things you have to do as a parent, they're probably not going to have a child. And I've actually talked to parents that have lost their loved ones. They have gone through it a lot longer than I had and they finally had this sensation of relief. I know it sounds ugly, but they felt like now the family can relax, take a sigh, a deep breath. Now they know that loved one is in a better place because during their addiction they were in hell and now, they're not.

Kimber Lynne: And you can sleep again.

Alan: Yeah.

Kimber Lynne: Were there times, because I know you go to sleep, you wake up at two or three in the morning, and the first thing you think of is why am I awake? Is she okay? Is she okay? Why am I awake? Or you're waiting for that phone call, and you know that phone call might come. And that phone call, we know what that phone call is.

Alan: Yeah. Well, yeah, I expected that anytime because I had so many people that I knew had gotten that phone call. You kind of go, "Well, it's going to happen" to the point you've been so tired so long that you had no positive thoughts ever. I'm going to treat you just like you are. It's not going to be nice, and I'm pretty sure you're going to die.

And so, I've come to the conclusion that I've done all I can do. And I've told parents that have lost their kids, you do realize you've done everything you could do. They tried to do everything they could do. They made mistakes along that line. But I mean, who's got a handbook for this?

Kimber Lynne: Tell me, tell everyone who reads "UnCut," what enabling is?

Timothy: Enabling is allowing them the latitude to do the things that are destroying them. The intentions are good; enablers don't have bad intentions. Enabling is, I want to help them. Well, we're getting to the point where we can no longer help them as a parent. There was a point where I couldn't help her anymore, but I was still going to. I knew what's best for my kid. We gotta face, sometimes we don't always know what's best for our kid. There's a world full of people with kids. Someone else has the answer for your kid that you don't have. And if enabling is trying to help but hurting then you need to stop. You're trying to help. You're gonna help your kid; you're not gonna hurt them. But enabling ultimately could kill them.

So, I'm going to give them the keys to the car and say, they gotta get to school. But they're not going to school. They're going to their buddies' house across the county. They need lunch; they're not spending that on lunch. You're giving them lunch money, and they're losing two pounds a week. Enabling is hurting when you're trying to help and being too blind to see that. It's still hurting and not helping. You have to realize there are things about your kid and addiction that you just don't know and you can't see it because it's your kid. I couldn't see it because it was my kid. I knew all about addiction because I've been an addict. But I couldn't see it, it would grab ahold, and I couldn't do anything about it.

Kimber Lynne: The other thing you said, which I believe because we lived it, there comes a time when you know what's going on but, you have to draw a line in the sand and be willing to lose them. And that's the hardest thing a parent can ever face.

Timothy: You gotta let go. You gotta let them go. My mother said this to me when she found out when I was using, she said, "Timothy, you know we love you, but you can't do that here. You can't do that here". I was popping pills and lying. You can't do that here. We're not going to let you stay here and do that. If you want to and I was old enough to make my own decision if you wanna do it, you do that, but we're not going to enable you to do it. My mother in love, I understand it now, in love, she let me go. She let me go.

5

The chemistry behind opioids and how it controls the brain
Diving into the "Why?"

▲▲▲

"If you take narcotics enough, it starts to deplete the dopamine in the brain at the synapse. Then you get to the point where you can't feel the pleasures of life."

▲▲▲

I know it's different for everyone, but for me, I wanted to understand why. I needed to know why this happens to some and not others. I wanted to understand, why they chase the high. I wanted to know why they can't just say "no." In this chapter, you'll go down that road with me and a pharmacist who tries in, laymen's terms, to explain how opioids affect the brain and how it changes the chemistry make up of an individual.

Kimber Lynne: What I'm looking for from a pharmacy

perspective is to understand how this national opioid crisis has become a daily newsworthy event. Why kids today, young adults, the people who are starting to maybe just play around with Percocet and things like that become addicted. How does that particular drug, or opioids in general, travel through the body and affect the brain, which tells these people, "I have to have it," tell me about the addiction part of this.

Joe Pike (pharmacist): There's a place in the brain, and it's called the pleasure center. Almost all of us have felt that pleasure center at one time or another. It could be that first cup of coffee in the morning or even the last Mountain Dew at the end of the day. Something happens there. We have neurotransmitters in the brain, and some of the basic ones are dopamine and epinephrine and norepinephrine. The center of this problem starts in the brain. You take a certain drug and it reaches that pleasure center in the brain and dopamine is released, one of the neurotransmitter, and you go, "Ah, that's what I needed, that's what I needed."

What happens with narcotics or opioids is that there are two types of people. There are some people who are prone, either their mental abilities or chemistry or whatever, to become addicts. And those are the people we see on TV being arrested. Those are the people who are living under the bridge. Those are the people who are just completely consumed to find and take that next drug.

The rest of us may not be that way. But if you take narcotics enough and it starts to deplete the dopamine in the brain at the synapse, then you get to the point where you can't feel good, happy. You can't feel the pleasures of life. You can't look out across a field of beautiful flowers and say, "Man, isn't that beautiful?" You become so intent on getting that dopamine release, and since you keep using it all up, you can't release, like you want it to, you just keep taking more drugs. It becomes a mental obsession.

But if you and I, normal people, I'll call myself normal, just for this interview. Normal people, when they start taking drugs, not to get high, but to relieve themselves of pain, they become what they call physically addicted. And as they're still depleting dopamine in the brain, they're still depleting the brain chemical, but they're not trying to get high. They're just trying to be normal. All of us can fall under that haze.

Don Smith, who fell down and broke his leg, was put on some real powerful opioids to relieve his pain. Maybe he took them for too long. Maybe he took them too close together, whatever, but when he runs out, he's going to go into withdrawal. He's going to feel bad, and as he takes those drugs, his level of pain will increase.

The pain level varies. Let's say you stump your toe. "Oh, that hurt." Well, if you keep taking narcotics for that or opioids (when you brush your foot across a nightstand at night), you're going to feel excruciating pain; because of the chemicals in the brain. There's not enough dopamine. There's not enough of your regular brain transmitter to tell you this is normal.

We don't ever want to get to the point where we don't feel pain. Pain is a protective mechanism. I touch the stove; I'm going to pull my hand back. You know, I'm not going to sit there and say, "Boy, that felt good. Let me try that again."

Kimber Lynne: If I'm understanding and I'm not sure I do, we naturally have dopamine that releases in our brain.

Joe Pike (pharmacist): That's true.

Kimber Lynne: So, when we take a narcotic, the natural dopamine turns off, and the narcotic takes over?

Joe Pike (pharmacist): No, actually what the narcotic does is it helps the synapse in the brain, that nerve synapse. The narcotic increases the need for dopamine and after using it for long periods of time, you deplete your own dopamine levels in the body. Where you're looking for that pain relief naturally from your dopamine to get relief it won't happen because it is not there anymore.

Kimber Lynne: Can it regenerate after you stop using?

Joe Pike (pharmacist): Yeah, it can, yeah.

Kimber Lynne: Is there a concrete time frame?

Joe Pike (pharmacist): No, that's an individual thing. I'm sure if I looked up in the right book somewhere, it would give an estimated time. It's just like most people who take short-term opioids will deplete their dopamine. They feel like, "I used to take one tablet to relieve my headache and now I have to take two." That type of thing. But the opioids, except for extreme cases, should be used for a short period of time.

What happened about 15 or 20 years ago, it started happening, some of the drug manufacturers started coming to doctors and say, "You have to treat pain aggressively." In other words, where we used to go to a dentist and have a tooth filled or whatever, he may have given us some Tylenol, maybe Motrin or Ibuprofen. They said, "That's not enough. You have to treat it aggressively. And if you don't treat it aggressively, they can sue you." And the scariest thing for a doctor or anybody in the health care profession is the word sue. Nobody wants that.

Kimber Lynne: Yeah.

Joe Pike (pharmacist): So, they kept pushing drugs that were much more potent and telling the physician, "You need to use it more aggressively. You don't want anybody to suffer from pain." Nobody wants to suffer from pain, but there's a difference between pain and discomfort, and that's, after having a couple of teeth filled, you have pain, and you probably have some discomfort. The difference what happens when you use it for long period of time, what used to keep you pain free, no longer can do that anymore. You have to take more. You have to change to something higher in a higher strength, or a different drug that's more powerful. And this is where this all started.

Kimber Lynne: Mm-hmm (affirmative).

Joe Pike (pharmacist): In the medical profession, there were some doctors that found out that if I give this person something really strong for pain, he'll come back to my office and then I can write him another prescription and charge him again. It became a money thing.

Kimber Lynne: So, it's a money thing? When did you, as a pharmacist filling scripts, say, "This is getting to be a lot? I'm seeing a lot of these narcotics flying off the shelf." Can you remember when you started paying attention to this and then maybe a red flag of thinking this could be a potential problem in the future?

Joe Pike (pharmacist): Well, not the true narcotic, the opioids were so sparingly given. Instead of someone needing to take a Percocet capsule or tablet, the doctor would have prescribed Motrin. They would have prescribed aspirin, whatever. Probably 20 years ago, and I walk into a pharmacy, a fairly busy pharmacy, I could take every narcotic, opioid narcotic in the pharmacy and place it down right there.

Kimber Lynne: And today?

Joe Pike (pharmacist): Usually, a narcotic prescription for pain, transient pain, would have been for maybe five or six days. Then all of a sudden, you started seeing this pain medication being prescribed for months. Where a normal prescription may have been 20 tablets, all of a sudden you saw prescriptions coming across the counter for 350 tablets.

That's when you started seeing the really bad stuff start happening. You had people who could not function without being or without taking narcotics. Their pain threshold had dropped so low that they were in pain every day and it was excruciating for them.

We would never, 20 years ago, unless you were someone who was terminally ill, who was in constant pain, you would never see narcotics given for more than two weeks. And all of a sudden, you see a prescription coming in for 350 really strong narcotic medication opioids for a month's supply. And it snowballed.

Now this person who is taking 350 narcotic tablets can't function normally in life. They have trouble holding a job. They have trouble doing what they're supposed to be doing to help feed their family. And they find out, "I can sell some of them." All right? It's the matter of groceries on the table. These people didn't start out being mean, degenerative, terrible people. They're now hooked on a medication and they're spending every dime they have to get that medication. They can't work. They can't function in society. To help them pay for their medication, they've cut back on theirs enough where they can sell some, and that might pay for the groceries. That may pay for the child's pair of shoes to go to school. It snowballed. I think we all have to realize there are a lot of Mikey's out there. If you remember the advertisement for Quaker Oats, "Let Mikey try it. He'll eat anything."

Kimber Lynne: Mm-hmm (affirmative).

Joe Pike (pharmacist): And there have always been a bunch of Mikey's out there.

Kimber Lynne: You're going right down the path I wanted you to go. The biggest misconception, with what you've just told me is that many say, "It was a choice. They can stop." You've heard it. It was a choice

Just say no. Just say no. Just stop. Just stop.

Joe Pike (pharmacist): Sure.

Kimber Lynne: For parents that may have a child or loved one and thinking, "Just quit." What do you tell them about why they can't just stop?

Joe Pike (pharmacist): Well, I try to let the people that I work with know that after someone has started going down that path and whether it was a quick path or slow path after they've gotten on that path, getting that next drug becomes everything they think about. "I want to get high."

And with narcotics, you don't get high; you get low. This encompasses their whole life. It didn't start out that way. It may have been Billy Joe down the street going through his mother's medicine cabinet and he took a pill out of a bottle. He took one and he thought, "Wow, that makes me feel good. Here, you try it." Mikey's already tried it now, so you try it. And he'll say, "Man, I never felt like that before."

We have misconceptions. It's like kids say, "I want to get high." They're not getting high; they're getting low. They're passing out; they're falling down on the floor. They can't breathe anymore. It's not a high.

Kimber Lynne: I only know what I was told when I had a major procedure, the Dr. said when you take those strong narcotic or opioids for pain, the heartbeat will actually slow down, correct? Tell me how it actually affects your heartbeat and breathing because people don't understand if you take too much what happens to them.

Joe Pike (pharmacist): The common effect of narcotics, yes, it stops pain. It also decreases respiration. Where you may be taking a breath every 20 seconds or so, you're just taking one every 10 or 20 seconds. You don't feel like you need to breathe. It decreases heart rate, so all that oxygenated blood circulating through your body is not getting there very well. Then you reach the point where you don't have enough oxygen in your blood. You don't feel like taking a breath. Now, that's hard to believe, but they don't. Sometimes you have to sort of wake them up, rub their chest bone. Do something to startle them enough where they take a breath. But as the narcotics increase in the blood system, you get to the point where you just quit breathing. You get to the point where your heart rate has dropped so low, you're not getting the blood circulation and oxygen to the blood, and you pass out.

But it doesn't stop when you pass out. It can get worse. Depending on how much you've taken, in time, it can get worse, and your heart stops. Or you've already passed out because you're not breathing and after a while, you die.

Kimber Lynne: Like we talked before, this has been going on for years, but people weren't dying like this?

What's the difference? The accessibility? More affluent?

Joe Pike (pharmacist): I don't think, it doesn't really have a whole lot to do with money. We say with alcoholics and with drug addicts, it can go from Park Avenue to park bench. It's not how good-looking you are, or whether you're ugly or not. It doesn't have anything to do with it. It's a person who has a tendency to have that compulsion to take the drug. It's not how many years you went to college or the fact that you didn't go to college and you had to work with your hands and the sweat of your brow every day. That doesn't make any difference.

One thing I want to explain, too, this problem's been going on for a long time. We thought it was a poor man's problem. It seemed that in a poverty-stricken area, they seemed to be using more drugs like that. And maybe they were trying to get out of themselves, to get out of this feeling of poverty. But most people, poverty is a strange thing.

I grew up where at one time in my life, I had two pairs of pants and two shirts. I got initiated into the varsity club in high school and part of that initiation, I had to climb a flagpole which happened to be on top of a brick pedestal. I climbed that flagpole. I climbed up that brick pedestal and when I did that, I ripped my pants. It wasn't one that you could just sew up. It was one of those tear type things. I went into the bathroom and sat down and cried. I only had two pairs of pants. Momma couldn't wash them and have them dry by the next morning. "What am I going to do?" That's poverty. But we also did a little farming. We grew some of our own food. We traded. I was never hungry.

So, it has nothing to do with poverty. It has nothing to do with riches. Here's a kid, the family's making a huge amount of money. They're living in some of the best homes in the whole world, but still, they took that pill and something lit in their brain and that pill became the most important thing in their life.

Kimber Lynne

Kimber Lynne: Why do you think, with all the advertisements right now, the president talking about it, the governor talking about it, it's all over the news, what's the fascination that people are still trying it? What are we doing wrong? What are we doing wrong in making them not want to try it?

Joe Pike (pharmacist): The problem with that particular part, you can tell a child, "Don't ever go into my medicine cabinet and take any of my medication. Don't ever do that." Because kids are experimenters. They want to see how hard they can hit that ball. They want to see what it takes to throw that pass down the field. And they experiment.

The only problem is these drugs are deadly to begin with. They have no knowledge, absolutely no knowledge of what they're taking except it makes them feel different. It's almost like an accident. "Oops, I didn't know it would do that."

Today we're dealing with drugs that our ancestors never thought about. These are some of these synthetic drugs like fentanyl. Why would anybody sell to anyone a drug that's going to drop their respiration, going to drop their heartbeat and will kill them because it feels good. It's my personal belief that that's an act of murder. One of the things we need to do is start enforcing the law.

Kimber Lynne: They've started.

Joe Pike (pharmacist): Yeah, they've started, but how many times do they get caught?

Kimber Lynne: Almost never?

Joe Pike (pharmacist): I have a thing, yeah, throw them in jail and throw the key away.

Kimber Lynne: Who?

Joe Pike (pharmacist): Drug dealers.

Kimber Lynne: Dealers? But the drug dealer is also the drug addict. Like you were saying, they live every day trying, "I've got to have it; my body's jumping. I'm going through withdrawals. You buy this. Now, I can get back to normal by taking some."

Joe Pike (pharmacist): But not all of them are.

Also, we have organizations that truly help with addiction and alcoholism, AA and NA. When you go to an NA meeting, how many people at that meeting are dealing?

Kimber Lynne: A lot?

Joe Pike (pharmacist): Yes.

Kimber Lynne: According to a relative who went to one, he says, "I go to these meetings, they're waiting outside the door to sell to me." They've got a captive audience right in front of them.

Joe Pike (pharmacist): Yeah, I've known enough of these guys. It's all about the all-mighty dollar. You can be an ignorant person, no college education, no qualifications of any type, but you can sell drugs today and drive the best car, wear the fanciest clothes, date the most beautiful women and that's another story. The pull is so hard.

Kimber Lynne: Parents. I would think that the parents of an addict are blaming themselves, "Where did I go wrong? What did I do wrong? I should have done this. I should have done that." Is there any way to ease their mind to say, "It really wasn't all you"?

Joe Pike (pharmacist): It's not all you, that's what the parent has to finally understand.

It's about any mother, not any, but most mothers and fathers will do anything for their children, anything. You see the children and you talk to them, but talking doesn't help a whole lot. "Why are you doing this? "Because my drive for doing this is more than my drive for success, good grades," whatever those goals are as you grow up, that drug is everything.

Does that mean they're a bad kid? No. I know some of the most wonderful young people in the world who are addicted to narcotics. What happened? Maybe it was Mikey. Maybe it was a guy that liked to try things. Maybe he's the guy who felt that he could play music a heck of a lot better when he was taking a pill or smoking a joint or whatever it was. "I'm better at it when I'm doing that."

And that's not unusual. You look at the music industry. Why did all these people end up drug addicts? Because it felt like they were free. They could play that next chord and the next chord, and it sounded better, and that was their joy in life. I don't know.

The parents didn't have anything to do with that. Their life that they're living right now is not because Momma put drugs in your veins. The mother and father loved them every bit as much as I have loved my children, every bit. There is a tremendous amount of guilt, and that's where Al-Anon, Narc-Anon, where you can go and be with other people in the same situation.

What about that husband that fell in love with this most beautiful woman? His heart was just completely taken away. Every minute of his day, even when he was fishing, but he wouldn't tell you that, though, he had thoughts of her. He loved her. And then, he sees you fading away. Your personality was changing. You're still beautiful, but you won't be long. It's like the kid thinks he's more talented when he takes that pill. And that's why it takes the actions of everybody when you sit down and say, "You're going to have to make a decision, son. You're going to have to have a little tough love. If you want to be a part of this group, you're going to have to change."

Kimber Lynne: Would you say, for any families dealing with the worst of the worse, right? It's under your nose. They're stealing; they're pawning, they're doing anything they can. They're stealing from you, all these things. Do you have to get to a point as a parent where you draw the line, knowing it's either going to help him, or I'm going to bury him?

Joe Pike (pharmacist): Well, sometimes, you've already come to that line. The drug takes you to that line. If he doesn't get better, he's going to die. You didn't make that. You didn't cause that. The addiction causes that. It's not

Kimber Lynne

because your son's a bad boy, it's because he's hooked on drugs. Most of these people, most of these young, beautiful, young people are not thieves. They don't normally break into houses and steal everything there is. They don't go through their Momma's jewelry case and pull out every bit of gold and whatever is there so they can sell it. That's not them. They've turned into that because of their addiction.

My goodness, I've had people in my family, and I think it's coming to the point where almost every family, somewhere in that family, there's somebody with that problem and you put your arms around them, and you hold them and tears come into your eyes. At that moment, that little child, that little child, maybe 25 years old, but that little child, your baby, is dying because of the way he's living. He's not just a bad boy. He's been taken over by drugs and alcohol.

Kimber Lynne: The stigma?

Joe Pike (pharmacist): The stigma's terrible.

Kimber Lynne: Talk about the stigma. How can we inform those that haven't experienced this addiction firsthand that they are making the situation worse by judging from the outside? All I know is that they had better be careful because there is a good chance it will hit home at some point. Right? There's a stigma.

Joe Pike (pharmacist): We love to be proud of our children. Isn't it great to go to a dinner party? You sit there and, "Yeah, old Joe is getting ready to go to Carolina this year, straight A's, of course. He's in pre-med. He's going to be the greatest doctor in the world." We all love to do that. We love to brag on our kids; whether he's the fastest runner in the school or whatever, we love bragging on our kids. We would like to take credit for some of it. "I was a great football player. That's why my son was a great football player." My problem was, I wasn't great, and my son was a great football player, who was also good at basketball. Anyway, we like to brag on our kids, and we all try to say, "Look what I've done to help that child be the best student, the best athlete," whatever.

But what can you brag about when your child's a drug addict? You say, "Did I cause that?" That's what's going through your mind. "What did I do to cause that? What could I have done differently to keep that from happening?" That's what you're working on today to find out what we do differently to keep that from happening.

The people I help in drugs and alcohol, whether that child is 45 years old, 50 years old, 60 years old, I'm still asking the same questions. "What can I do? What can I say to turn that person around?" I hope somebody finds that secret word. Love's a lot to do with it. Don't quit loving yourself because when you don't take care of yourself, you can't help others. Don't quit loving.

6

THE DANGEROUS DRUG COCKTAIL THAT KILLS WITHOUT INTENT

▲▲▲

"It was terrifying. I remember watching the monitor and seeing my heart rate, seeing my pulse. At one point, I remember it being 226 beats a minute."

▲▲▲

You only really know what you hear in the news or what you read as a headline or the tragic stories of overdoses killing a friend of a friend or a friend's child. It is hard to understand why someone would concoct a mixture of opioids with other things like fentanyl to expedite the euphoria faster. You immediately call it criminal. The entirety of the crisis is overwhelming and beyond comprehendible. Much like everything in life, if you are not affected by addiction, you have a very hard time understanding why someone would ever do this to themselves. During the interview with Timothy, he talks about drug use as being the same as it related to using. What he said was different was the mixing of drugs. He does not recall the unknown potency of street drugs in the '60s and '70s.

Kimber Lynne: So, back then, when you were using in the '60s – no fear of dying? Was there any talk of addiction?

Timothy: Oh, no, no. Addiction as far as any that serious is more associated with heroin back in the '60s and '70s. Drug addicts were the heroin junkies. Snatch purses or die in the alleys, you know. Era of, yeah, it was like the groovy era. I guess still some people from Vietnam. You hear about Vietnam veterans being messed up. Heroin was a serious thing. There were serious drugs around, but heroin was the drug addict, addict, drug. Reefer? Harmless. Cocaine was very recreational. Almost, like, zero problem associated with cocaine back then, you know. It was recreational, and it made you, I don't know, laughy and happy. And you snort a little bit, and there was, you know, no repercussions.

Kimber Lynne: You make reference to, back then. When we talk about the drug (heroin), you know, we think about the '60s and the '70s. As you look back then and forward to today, is there a bigger drug problem today than back then? Is it the same and we're just more informed because the media's telling us more about it?

Timothy: It's the same. It's the same that, I mean, back in the '60s and '70s the term was, junkies, dying in alley; like a Rolling Stones song. You know, the girl put a needle in her arm, died in the dirt of the alleyway. It was a die in the streets drug back then. Today, modern technology, if something happens, anywhere, you hear about it instantly. So, it's not new, it's just a different era; same stuff. Of course, now it seems to be more potent and deadly, especially with that Fentanyl thing. They didn't have Fentanyl back then. If you just wanted to get super high like that, you just did more and overdosed.

▲ ▲ ▲

Robert Nelson is a policeman whom I interviewed about the difficulty of being on the front line every day dealing with the effects of opioids and other drugs. Nelson is young in his early '30s and working in a small town. If you really want to know how bad the problem is you can go ask your local EMS or law enforcement and I promise you that you will be shocked at what you hear.

Kimber Lynne: You're on the streets. How bad is it? This problem?

Robert Nelson (Police Officer): It's a problem that, in all honesty, I wasn't exposed to it much before I was a police officer. It was sort of this thing that it happened to a few kids that I knew in high school. It happened to a friend's cousin. It wasn't something that I saw every day. Now, it's something that we deal with on a weekly basis. Maybe not overdoses, but addicts, users, dealers. It's things we see weekly, if not daily and as to whether or not the problem has grown or lessened over the years, I'm not sure, but I will say that the problem, itself is massive. It doesn't just affect the people using; it affects their families. It affects police officers; it affects medical staff; it affects your friends and your loved ones. It affects the people that still care about you, and if you choose to start using, if you choose to go down that road, you're going to be destroying more lives than your own with this problem.

Kimber Lynne: We used to say this problem is in the lower socioeconomic class. Can you group it into one class today?

Robert Nelson (Police Officer): I don't think you can group it into one class or one age group or one race or one anything. The people that I've dealt with this problem, it's been in every neighborhood, every walk of life, every race, every gender. It really doesn't discriminate. I had somebody talking to me about it refer to it as a disease, and diseases don't discriminate. The flu doesn't care if you have money, it doesn't care if you're white or black or Asian, the flu just kind of hits you and it puts you down, and opioids and other abusive substances are the same way. Once you catch them, once you get ahold of them, they're gonna put you down, and it doesn't matter where you come from or who you are, it's just gonna hurt.

Kimber Lynne: I heard it said that there are two roads if you're gonna use.

Robert Nelson (Police Officer): Yeah. In all honesty, if you use and you're not one of the lucky ones to get out, because it doesn't always have to do with personal anything whether or not you get out, sometimes it's just your situation but if you use and you continue to use, you're either gonna end up behind bars, or you're gonna end up in the

Kimber Lynne

ground. Somebody's either gonna arrest you for possession, or you're gonna end up dealing yourself to fuel your habit and you're gonna end up in prison, or you're not gonna be lucky enough to have someone save you and you're gonna end up in a box in the ground.

Kimber Lynne: You were called to a scene, and you were exposed to a substance. Tell me how that went down, what happened, how did you feel, how long were you suffering?

Robert Nelson (Police Officer): It started off as a pretty standard drug activity call. Once we got to the scene, we took the substance from the subject we'd been called to investigate. During our search of where we'd been called to, I was exposed to trace amounts of the substance. About 45 minutes after we had finished searching, I was vomiting profusely and had to be transported to the hospital for emergency care.

I was told I spent about 13 hours there. I was awake for about five of those, and to be honest, it was terrifying. I remember watching the monitor and seeing my heart rate, seeing my pulse. At one point, I remember it being 226 beats a minute. They had to take me in for a CAT scan to make sure my heart wasn't going to explode. I'd never been through anything like that before. I've been in a lot of situations that have made me sweat, and this was one that I, looking back on it, I wasn't sure I was walking out of without some sort of major issue.

It took me four days afterward to be able to actually get up and do things normally. I had stomach issues; I had muscles issues. I had actually pulled a muscle in my neck from vomiting so hard, and it took me about a week and a half afterward for everything to kind of go back to normal.

It came back later that what I was exposed to was a mix of heroin, fentanyl, cocaine, and some other chemicals, and what we had been told by the people on the scene was that it was just heroin and it goes to show kind of you have no idea what is in this stuff and what you're getting exposed to. Even just being around it can be dangerous and extremely hazardous to your health.

Kimber Lynne: So, you had told me prior to turning the camera on that when you got to the scene, and you realized what exactly you were doing, you put gloves on.

Robert Nelson (Police Officer): I did. Once we realized what we were dealing with, I did put gloves on. One thing that as a police officer, what we are taught about fentanyl is that it'll actually eat through our nitrile gloves. When it comes to the patches of the chemical itself, we're taught that it'll eat through clothing, it'll come through gloves and cause exposures that way, and it can also be inhaled. One way, people are introducing these chemicals into their body is an inhalant. They're snorting it through straws or smoking it, so if you get exposed to the powder and you breathe that in and that can lead to the devastating effects that I went through.

▲ ▲ ▲

Fentanyl is a synthetic opioid between 50 to 100 times more potent than morphine. The drug is prescribed for severe pain, but is increasingly being sold on the street, many times mixed with heroin or other drugs. Fentanyl is so powerful that it poses a threat to emergency service staff who encounter it as part of their job. Inhaling just a few airborne particles or brushing the particles from a uniform could be fatal.

Kimber Lynne: Pretty scary stuff knowing that people do this intentionally?

Robert Nelson (Police Officer): It's terrifying. Having talked to people that have done this intentionally, that have brought themselves to that point in their life, I can't imagine how that could become a routine part of your life – not knowing what you're putting into your body and risking that kind of pain and prolonged suffering that you're going to go through.

Kimber Lynne: I'm gonna switch gears a little bit. Your job will put you in places where you see addicts close to death. Kind of walk me through the call and how that happens. I mean, you're a police officer, but you're a person, too. You could probably put a friend from high school on that ground or a relative or something. You are looking at a person, not just, hey, this is my job.

Robert Nelson (Police Officer): In some ways, I don't have too. A lot of times, we have friends and family there on scene and, if they're not there at the time, they show up pretty shortly after, whether it's in the hospital or somewhere else and their distress is immense. The users, the addicts themselves often break down into tears and discuss how they got to that point, because it's so disparaging to them and they don't like to talk about that.

Something that eats at me a little bit, as a police officer is when I get on scene and somebody is purple, and I don't mean that as a term, I mean that as an actual color. When somebody is so blue in the skin because they are not breathing and we administer Narcan, and we bring them back, we don't know what we're bringing them back from. A lot of people can be terrified and we do actually sometimes end up having to restrain people that are brought back, because they have had a near-death experience and they're terrified. And so, sometimes we end up having to restrain them with handcuffs or medical restraints and watch them work through mentally what's just happened to them.

Other times, I can remember instances where we've administered Narcan and we get them breathing and the people that are there, friends, family, something like that, just literally lose their feet (fall to the ground) because they thought they had just watched a loved one die. Having personally watched a loved one die, that is not something that is easy to take.

Kimber Lynne: You know, people who might read this and they're thinking Narcan's gonna save me 100% of the time, does it fail?

Robert Nelson (Police Officer): I'm not a medical professional. I don't like to talk about things I'm not as educated in as others. As far as the effectiveness of Narcan, when I've seen it administered properly, it has worked. What I will say is that Narcan is not always gonna be there. You're having to put your trust of your life, the trust that you will live through this in someone else's hands and unless you've developed an extreme level of trust with them, that's not something you want to do.

Kimber Lynne: Especially if, say you're waiting to take turns. If you're gonna say, "I'll go, if something happens, you use Narcan and then you'll go and if something happens, I'll use Narcan on you." Well, that's a terrible system.

Robert Nelson (Police Officer): So, if somebody who's able to administer Narcan isn't there or if you just don't have Narcan, to begin with, it's not gonna save your life. In all honesty, you need to know that Narcan has an effective time period. We're told it's about an hour. So, if after that hour you're not constantly monitored, say you've gotten your Narcan, you go to the hospital, you're fine, and you walk out, and after an hour you still have it in your system, and it wears off, you could fall out right there. I've personally talked to some medical professionals, some EMT's that have seen it happen. They'll go to the same person three or four times in one night because the Narcan and naloxone will wear off and they'll lapse right back into where they were before it was administered.

▲ ▲ ▲

The trickle-down effect is far more widespread than any of us can imagine. Many addicts become addicted after procedures that had Percocet prescribed for pain. Wisdom teeth, athletic injuries, back pain, all of which could contribute to the need and sometimes they want to use. I interviewed a pain management doctor that explains how the body misinterprets pain after the continuous use of pain medications.

Kimber Lynne: I am going to get right to the heart of this deal. Did you see this coming? This epidemic?

Dr. Kirk Harum (Pain Management Doctor): I didn't see it. No. But in retrospect, it's easy to see. As far back as the late 90's the marketing for pain medicines, opioids, seemed to increase, and the prescribing also increased. In general, the doctors overall seem to increase the dosage because the mantra was often, if you're still hurting, just increase the pain medicine, and that was before many of us knew of the harmful effects of opioids. Now, there are many known bad effects of opioids other than addiction. They include common side effects, like nausea, vomiting, constipation, weight gain interference, and immunity, and of course, the one that we all know about is addiction. One of the things that are important to distinguish in addiction is addiction from physical dependence due to tolerance. A lot of times, these things are confused by patients and often confused by physicians. So, addiction is a behavior that is harmful to the patient or to the person where they will do things like taking opioids when they know that they're harmful for them and for no particular medical benefit. A lot of patients will come in and say I think I'm addicted to this medicine, and what they've really developed is tolerance, and tolerance is a common physiologic problem with opioids right now. I could prescribe a person, you know, one Percocet pill twice a day, and their pain is well controlled. But six weeks, eight weeks, later they might need three or four, and that is a normal physiologic response or could be a normal physiologic response called tolerance. Another normal physiologic response that is often confused with addiction is physical dependence. Physical dependence happens with opioids and many other drugs, including antihypertensives and antidepressant medications. It just means that if you were to spot the drug suddenly, the patient would go through withdrawal symptoms, which may include feeling jittery, feeling nauseous, sweating, difficulty with sleep, and other symptoms.

Kimber Lynne: The government in North Carolina has been proactive and has stepped in to help control the prescription amount that doctors can prescribe. What is this law?

Dr. Kirk Harum (Pain Management Doctor): Yes. The stop law.

Kimber Lynne: Explain for those that aren't in this nightmare, what is the stop law?

Dr. Kirk Harum (Pain Management Doctor): The stop law is a law passed by the North Carolina legislature, which went into effect in January of 2018. For example, if a patient were to come in with a new acute onset of pain, a physician is only allowed to prescribe five days-worth of pain medicine. If that patient required additional care for their pain, they would need to be reassessed by the same physician or another physician. At that point, they could be prescribed a longer, if appropriate, prescription for opioids. It also puts a seven-day limit on prescriptions for patients who have had surgical procedures or other interventions in a medical setting, and the same rule applies that the patient would need to be reassessed after seven days before they receive additional pain medicine.

Kimber Lynne: Have we become as a society soft in dealing with pain?

Dr. Kirk Harum (Pain Management Doctor): I believe it was in the 1990s when Medicare began to have medical personnel monitor what they called the "fifth" vital sign, and that was your pain level. Patients were asked on a scale of 1-10 with zero being no pain and 10 being the worst pain you could ever have, how bad is your pain? This scale was included in all of the medical interactions with patients, whether they were complaining of pain or not. I think that kind of led to some changes as well. Somewhere in the '90s, there was an editorial letter to the editor where a physician, I can't remember his name, stated that in his experience, there were no ill effects from long-term opioid therapy, and things kind of took off from there. His letter to the editor was quoted many many times as support from prescribing opioids to patients.

Kimber Lynne: What's the most difficult thing that you have to deal with now being a pain management clinic? You have people with real issues who are being affected because of the misuse of opioids and other pain meds, where do you draw the line? How do you deal with that?

Dr. Kirk Harum (Pain Management Doctor): That's a difficult one for all Physicians, not just pain management. We are trained to believe the patient, but quite honestly, we probably spend a good deal of mental energy trying to figure out if a patient is legitimate or not. We do use screening tools. We have something called an opioid risk tool. We have access to psychological intervention and evaluation. We do urine drug screening to evaluate the patients. We have the opportunity to look into the North Carolina controlled substance registry to see if patients have been prescribed opioids by other doctors. These are a lot of tools that we did not have ten years ago, and back then, we were often fooled by a patient who seemed legitimately honest, and they are just not being honest with us. We would write them a prescription for opioids and find out later that they had just gotten a similar prescription a day earlier from a different doctor. So today, it's a little bit easier to keep track of what patients are prescribed. One of the problems with the controlled substance registry is that it doesn't cross state lines in most instances. This becomes very difficult for physicians that are in border towns where a patient can cross from one state to another after receiving a prescription.

7

OVERCOMING SHAME

▲▲▲

"It got to the point that I couldn't even go find anybody that didn't have a loved one or knew of a loved one who was not going through this."

▲▲▲

It takes a while to overcome the stigma attached to the family that has a drug addict. And the stigma carries more weight when the addiction escalates to what one of my interviews had labeled as a super addict, which correlated to "heroin."

As you begin to unravel the details and the severity of the addiction, your social circles become much smaller.
During the pre-driving years, you shared benchmarks of successes, accolades, new girlfriends, or boyfriends. After all, your children are your greatest achievement.

They carry your "DNA." My husband and I are overachievers. I am hopeful that we are well thought of in our community.

Kimber Lynne

My husband has a great job and is beloved by the people he works with and for. He is a God-fearing Christian whose heart is the size of Texas (maybe larger). He serves in the church. He coaches and mentors the youth. He supports junior athletics and its growth. I am active in the church and philanthropic work as well. Our goal is to be great examples for all of our children and make sure that they have the best opportunity for success. With that being said, we both believe that maybe we missed the mark. Perhaps our dedication to being good stewards in our community took away moments in time that our children required. Perhaps we missed their pain. Maybe they didn't share their internal struggles. Well, I believe you can't move forward if you stay in the past. I actually heard earlier tonight in a meeting about recovery that there is the rule of three C's. It's not exactly how it was said, but the gist of it is; You can't change what happened, you didn't cause it, and You can't control it. They are spot on. It's true, but it takes a long, long time to get to that point as a parent.

I remember several years ago a friend calling me on the phone. Our child was a first-year student playing division 1 athletics at a University. Somehow, they had received information that our child was seen using cocaine at a party on campus. Their child wasn't even enrolled at this University. How could they have this information? Who saw what and shared it with them? My friend wanted to meet with my husband and me as soon as we had time. Well, I immediately asked what was wrong. They said we needed to meet them in person. Now I knew something was up. I said, "Is it about one of my children?" Yes. So, I said, "Just tell me right now what is going on." Reluctantly, they told me what they had heard. My first thought was to say thank you. I know many people would have avoided calling us thinking they may be risking a friendship. I headed straight to my husband's workplace and called him to his office. I explained the phone call and pleaded to leave immediately and drive to the University unannounced to confront the situation. It couldn't be true, I thought. My child is a scholarship athlete. I know they drug test. There must be some mistake. He agreed that we needed to drive, as long as it would take and surprise our child with a drug test in hand. It was a long ride and when we finally arrived, surprised our child. "Why are you here?" "It's the middle of the week." We began by asking how everything was going. How are your classes? How is your living situation with your roommates? How is it going with your coach? All the things you are supposed to ask to let your child know you are vested in their life. You truly care about what is going on. Then my husband grabbed him and gave a bear hug with the words, "You know how much we love you?" Then we got to the reason we were there. We asked for a drug test to be taken while we were there. Of course, there was a hodgepodge of excuses as to why that wasn't going to happen. Things like I just went to the bathroom. I don't have to go. I don't have a drug problem why are you asking me to take a drug test when the University randomly tests their athletes? So, we ensured that we had all day. We would sit there all day until there was a need to urinate. We weren't leaving until it happened. Quickly there was an appointment to turn in a paper on campus and our firstborn said they would return. We sat together, wondering how long we would have to wait. Of course, my mind went to him looking for someone who might know how to beat a drug test. Is there an over the counter drug that could block the traces of cocaine or any other illegal substance that could be in the bloodstream? Eventually, we administered the test, and it came back negative. What a relief, right? My friend was misinformed. It was some other kid that looked like my kid – a case of misidentification.

Kimber Lynne

We started home and didn't say much. I was still suspicious and believed that we failed at getting the entire story. There wasn't enough transparency in his explanation of why we were told what we had been told.

Oh yeah, when they ask you who gave you the information, under no circumstances do you tell! You need your intel and you can't muddy the relationship of coughing up names as proving the integrity of your source.

Back to the stigma, of course, we called our friend and thanked them again for loving us enough to share what they had heard but let them know that we didn't think it was true because we had traveled and confirmed a negative drug test result. I don't think over the next eight years it was ever brought up again. So, I don't know if they just decided at that point not to meddle or that our child was more careful not to let anything happen around kids they grew up with.

You have to pay attention to changes in behavior. Look into their eyes. What do you see? Are they sluggish when they usually have energy? Do they have an overabundance of energy where they can't sit still? How is their appetite? There were a few ups and downs through the rest of college, but a minor outpatient surgery probably was the beginning of understanding how heavy narcotics can give a euphoric escape that our son had never experienced before. I suppose there were anxieties over a relationship breakup, the stress of finishing school, the thoughts of pursuing a dream in the career world.

The fear of disappointing us. So, I am confident there was a consistent and functioning drug use that occurred for many years. There was anger. There was frustration over situations that really didn't warrant the intensity or level it escalated to. I found marijuana paraphernalia in the drawer when putting away laundry and I challenged the explanation. Of course, he said it wasn't his. There were lighters that continually showed up in the wash. I asked, "Why do you need a lighter?" There were friends that showed up smoking in my driveway or smoking out back on the deck. I immediately expressed my displeasure with that whole scene. So, were the signs there? You bet. Could we stop it back then? Knowing what I know now, we could have shortened the trip to get our child to rehab. The car they were driving was in our name. We allowed him to live in our house after graduation while trying to build a future. We paid the cell phone bill, the car insurance. We put food on the table and in the house. Bottom line, we enabled! If any of this is mirroring your current situation, then hopefully, you can get your loved one to recovery faster by knowing what we and the transcripts included have gone through.

Eventually, we started challenging behavior and stories that just didn't add up. If the story doesn't make sense and the pieces don't add up, then it is probably not the truth. For example, using your debit card to go get gas 20 miles away when there is a gas station right around the corner. If you needed gas, why not go to the closest one? The behavior of locking doors, like the bathroom door or always running water when in the bathroom, like the shower or the sink, making frequent trips out to the car in the driveway, being alert one moment, and then sleeping a lot. Slowly, removing themselves from social scenes with friends. Once we were really paying attention and requesting drug tests (that were always refused) our child started to find a job as far away as possible.

The job opportunity came and was a six-hour drive from where we lived. A new start we had hoped. Newly, driven to succeed and leave the using behind? Well, you already know that was not the case. No one monitoring and the ticking time bomb was just a matter of time. I ask, is it better not knowing, not seeing it go on right in front of you? I think it might be worse. You always wonder how bad it is and will you get the same call that some parents of drug addicts have received.

There were moments of hope in the first six months, but there was also evidence that the using was still going on, always chasing money. Can I borrow some cash, "I'll pay you back next week type of thing"? Living with one roommate and saying they were the problem and making their life miserable and having to move. I could hear moments of fear at times over the phone. One night I got a call and I realized after hearing the cry for help in his voice that the timing was right to hold an intervention. My child was crying out for help and I knew, he knew, it had now become out of his control. I got off the phone and went to my husband and within hours we had contacted three of the strongest Christian men in our family that we knew had some influence over our child and pleaded for them to help.

The next day, we met at the closest airport hub near our intervention site. You have to listen carefully to what your child is saying. Timing is everything. We got a hotel room, and one of the uncles enticed the meeting, saying he was in town on business. This was one of the most difficult things I've ever witnessed. There was prayer. There was love. There were tears. After two hours, we loaded our child up and drove all night long to a rehab center we had found in another state. The 28-day program had started. I thanked God for this step in recovery. I had been praying to God every night and day and sometimes more. I would wake up in the middle of the night and asked him if he woke me up because my child was in trouble. Why was I awake? This occurred a lot in 2 years. I used to pray, "God, please save my child. Please keep my child safe." Finally, I realized that was not the prayer I should have been praying. I changed it to, "God, please take the desire to use away from my child. Please change the power of the drug over him and to his brain."

You go through so much dealing with this and trying to solve the addiction and trying to fix it. You don't share your struggle with anyone outside the family. The immediate family is on an island trying to get through each day one minute at a time. You wonder how it will end. Will this treatment center cure the disease? But you realize you are not alone. Bill is a parent that, like all of the others, watched his child go in and out of treatment facilities. He and his wife endured years of manipulation, lying, and stealing. Both kept the dark secret inside the doors of their home, hoping that no one would find out and judge them.

> *Bill:* I never told anyone in my family until I had to. I was ashamed of it for her, and we never brought it outside of the family. Now that she has recovered, I've not talked any more about it. I've never gone into any great detail with it. You sort of start isolating the whole family because it's – protect the kids. We didn't want anybody else to know about it, and we didn't know when she was going to have one of her episodes. Our social life went to hell in a handbasket because you want to keep it totally in the family.

▲▲▲

Kimber Lynne

The 28 days went by and we were able to have contact by a landline once a week for a short period. It was great and it sounded like the child we knew. At the end of the 28 days, it was a return back to where they had been living and back to work. Healthy and with some new tools to survive the real world and the pressures that came with it. We were so proud of the accomplishment that we provided some "get started money" and once again, had the car fixed that had been wrecked several times. We believed it was all behind us. As it turned out, using again was just hours away after being discharged. A couple of months had passed and a friend of our child's called at 10 pm. She wanted to know if she could come by the house. I said, "Right now?" She said yes, and I, of course, said, "come on." I knew something was terribly wrong. She was terrified of what she had seen when visiting and began crying. The story was heartbreaking for us and we knew that it wasn't just pills anymore. I believe she saved the life of our child and I will be forever grateful for the strength it took to tell us what she had discovered. We convinced our child that they needed to return home so that we could work on this as a family. He believed that by locking himself in the house with no access to a phone or a vehicle, he could get back on track and never use again.

When you are as addicted as our child was, it was inevitable that there would eventually be a run-in with the law. And it happened. Facing a possible felony charge, DUI, we were advised to go back to the first rehab center and get help. This time it culminated in 56 days of therapy, meetings, and volunteer work at a local church. Then it was recommended that the next step would be a bed in a recovery house for over a year and a half. This time it was our child's decision, not a decision to please the parents. We missed our first Thanksgiving and Christmas with our son, but in our heart, we knew it was the only way to have a chance at beating this.

My husband was facilitating a holiday party at his employment during this time and rumors had started to emerge. Right after the run-in with the law, a mug shot appeared in the local paper, so it was hard to hide at this point. You knew people were looking at you differently. I avoided holiday parties because frankly, I just didn't want to answer any questions. We had been through a terrible time. But on this night of my husband's work party, the stigma was lifted because he went after it head-on. In front of about 80 people, he spoke, informing them that our child was a drug addict and was in a rehab center in another state. He said he would hope that they wouldn't talk among themselves as facts get misstated when that happens. He asked that everyone pray for our child and our family. So there. We addressed it publicly so as to defuse rumors. He said if anyone had any questions at all to please come to us privately. What was amazing about this was over the next several months' people who had heard the news had come to talk to us about the very same problem in their home. I'm not talking one or two families, there were multiple, and they felt safe talking to us and hoping that we could give them some direction. The stigma, yes, still exists for those who are uneducated. But when you accept the disease for what it is, only then do you free yourself from any judgment from other family members, friends, or acquaintances.

Kimber Lynne: The stigma when someone comes up and says, "Hey Alan, how's your daughter doing?" They have no clue what you've been going through.

Alan: It was there, but I was really willing to tell it, and it was kind of ironic that the more I would tell these other people would tell me it was either in their family or out of family, or they knew somebody. And it got to the point that I couldn't even go find anybody that didn't have a loved one or knew of a loved one who was not going through this. So, the stigma, I just, what the heck. I just let that go. I quit enabling. Quit worrying about what other people thought. Quit worrying about what she thought. My sole goal was to go out and find somebody that could help her after that.

8

WHICH REHABILITATION CENTER IS RIGHT FOR YOUR LOVED ONE?

▲▲▲

"You have to get involved in your own life."

▲▲▲

Brent Brotos (recovered addict Wilmington, NC): I've been in recovery for four and a half years. I've been clean and sober. I originally left North Carolina four and half years ago and sought treatment in California at Tree House Recovery in Portland, Oregon, which now I work for as the Physical Empowerment Director. What we're doing out there is completely different than anything that I've ever seen before. I know that it doesn't exist out here and it needs to. The entire nation needs to take a look at the biological and social components of the disease and ask themselves, "Are we really treating this?" Because oftentimes from what I've seen in the past is a lot of focus on the psychological without too much focus on the biological and the social. Going back to the program and what has worked for me. I had to transform my entire lifestyle. So, fitness, martial arts, Navy seal style training on the beach and yoga have all become a part of my life. They're part of the program that I went through and the program that I work for now and it worked for me and it's working for a lot of people. These days I know and understand the importance of physical activity and the fact that I've been educated on why it's important, how it can defeat or tackle mental health disorders, not just addiction but anxiety, depression, and ADHD. It can release the same chemicals in your brain that you get from prescription drugs that you might be taking to combat those issues.

So, understanding and having an education on the importance of those things, of physical activity, and also the importance of social connection is critical. Oftentimes in addiction, we are isolated. We're shut down. Not just from the community but from ourselves too. And we feel alone, we don't feel connected. We don't feel a part of that and that's an important piece. Removing the stigma of addiction and taking that away so that we can take a deeper look at the individual as a human who's struggling, who is suffering, who has been through traumas from their past from family related issues, most likely. Environmental related issues, all of these factors have to be addressed and considered when treating the addict, the pills and the prescriptions. I think we need to take a look and the entire nation needs to take a look at lifestyle, biology's role in addiction, the social component and the psychological and ask ourselves, are we truly treating these things?

Kenny Houser (Coastal Horizons, NC): I think it's important when people talk about the recovery journey they're on, to realize that there are a lot of paths to recovery.

Medications, whether they're the FDA approved medications, methadone, buprenorphine, or naltrexone are all very effective with different individuals in different populations. And there are others who find recovery without those medications and there's a lot of in-between. And there's a wide continuum of how people get well. And I think one of the most important things to realize is that we need to make everything available for people to find recovery.

The medications that are helpful, as well, as the other behavioral supports, as well, as peers that can walk alongside of them, as well as, their families and that faith community. All of that plays a part in that. And I don't think we need to focus so much on which path of recovery or which medication but make whatever's available that'll help people find recovery. That's where we're headed. We're not headed for one thing or another. We're headed for recovery where many people can find that journey successfully in different ways.

Recovery is a very courageous journey. And we heard about reducing stigma, we talked about this a year ago, that when stigma goes down so that people are more free to get help and talk about the things they're struggling with, that the hope goes up. And we need to increase hope at all different levels so that people who take this courageous journey into recovery are fully supported and not shamed by that. That's why I'm so glad that we're actually talking about real stories. So, we've got to support this courageous journey of recovery to increase the hope.

Kimber Lynne: Backtracking, just a couple of quick questions. Finish this sentence: 28 days, 56 days, or even three

Kimber Lynne

months doesn't work in recovery. Like when you first go to treatment, does a 28-day program work with a heroin addict?

Brent Brotos: Our program is five months. Yeah. A 30-day program does not work. A 30-day program or I would say two or three weeks is good enough to stabilize somebody so that they can move to a different level of care. But basically, if you are trying to achieve treating that individual and healing every single past experience, every single past trauma, rebuilding them physically, it can't be done in 30 days. It's not realistic. And it doesn't make sense on a neurological level to recondition their entire brain in just 30 days. PAWS or Post-Acute Withdrawal Syndrome can last up to two years. So that should tell you that even with a five-month-long program, the client still needs up to two years of consistent work on themselves to make sure that they're restoring their brain back to a normal level of functioning. Now, when you implement exercise, I think it does speed up the process, but I don't know the actual data. All I know is that it takes two years, up to two years before those symptoms disappear.

▲ ▲ ▲

Recently I attended an open house for a newly established multi-year treatment center for addiction. The room was filled with at least 45 individuals who were given an invitation to attend for the purposes of raising money to open the doors. During that hour the attendees were asked by a show of hands if they knew anyone who was struggling with addiction. The answer was an overwhelming yes. Every single person in the room raised their hand. It was also evident that some attending had a personal experience with addiction either from their own battle or with a loved one. Because of this, there were many opinions on what type of recovery program actually works. There were concerns about whether or not you should have to pay to receive therapy and treatment. What is not long enough, and what is too long as it relates to months or years of treatment? Should alternative medication assist in the treatment of opioid addiction?

Kenny Houser (Coastal Horizons, NC) said it best that there is no cookie-cutter treatment. Everyone is different, and when you combine the mental side of addiction, it becomes very individual. Most of the addicts I interviewed went multiple times to a rehabilitation center, hoping to find the tools of never using again. Most of these addicts were trying the 28-day to 3-month model of treatment. So, this small Beta group has proven that it does take longer than what a short-term facility provides.

> *Alan:* I think that I've asked my daughter, I said, "Do you still have the sensation to do this again?" And she said, "Yes." She said, "It's a constant battle, the fight." It's something that I can't understand and don't want to ever understand, but it's in their brain at this point in time. This "feel good" gained from using is at risk of happening again for let's say a breakup of a boyfriend or losing a job, anything can set it off. You're scared of that because you've had people that you know that there are kids who had gone to rehab one, two, three times at different places and come back home on Christmas and overdose and die.
>
> So, you always have that fear, I mean, my daughter's been clean for going on two years now, but I still don't trust her

any. It's one of those things; I don't trust her to tell me the truth. You've lost trust, and it's not going to be there. It's probably going to take a long, long time to ever get that trust back. But in the back of your mind you're kind of going, well, if it happens, it happens.

And I told my daughter when I threw her out; I said, "I know in my heart, my conscience that I have done all I could do. Now the rest is up to you." I said, "This is something I can't do for you." I said, "So get out and don't come back." And it sucked. A lot of people don't do that. And your choices are to be ugly, tough love, or either you're going to be burying your child. Our daughter went through her first rehab just to get us off her back. Didn't do a bit of good, wasted a lot of money and a lot of them go through this three or four times. You have to go through it long-term. Most of them are six weeks or two months. I told my daughter that some of these programs are actually two years long. And one of the things that is good about those programs is they don't bring that child back into that same environment. Many stories you hear are they go home and call a friend. "Well, let's go and drink." And the next thing you know, they're doing drugs. So yeah, they need a long-term program.

Diane: And I realized, one day, I just didn't want to do it anymore. It was just like, I don't want to do it.

I just don't have the desire to and that was when I realized that my boyfriend at the time had this full-blown addiction because it became not an option for me anymore. My relationship became emotionally, verbally, and physically abusive. So, I was forced to sell everything I had and buy drugs.

Sorry, it's kind of hard to talk about. One thing led to another, and basically, it was a total of six months of me having fun and, you know, just playing around. And before I knew it, I had a full-blown addiction that I couldn't control.

I tried to, you know, stop on my own. I tried my own in-house rehab. This is six months in of a pill addiction. I stayed in my house for a total of 14 days, and my dad tried to help me. He kept me in the house, too and the 15th day when I got out of my house, I immediately went and got high. And the reason was because I was 19 and I had an opiate addiction. The hardest thing about detoxing is that withdrawals come with it and certain things happen to your body. One that was really bad for me was diarrhea, things like that. So, at 19 years old, to make it really in your face, I shit on myself at 19 and that was just it for me.

I was furious, but I was like screw it. I'm going to get high because, you know, that was 14 days in and I should have been over it by then. The withdrawals, the physical addiction and this is happening to me on day 14! I was just pissed off. So, I've always kind of been rebellious my whole life. So, I guess I just kind of rebelled. I think it comes from being an only child, you know. So, anyways what it comes down to is I ended up having a nine-year addiction to opiates and like I said, the first six months was just kind of playing around.

You know first, it was having fun and then it was, you know, I got myself into a situation that I didn't know how to get out of. And before I knew it, I was battling this addiction that I had no idea where it was going to take me. So, I mean, I was really naïve. I had no idea what I got myself into, not a clue.

When I was on pills, I did pills for about six years and I would snort them. You know, dealing with the whole addiction thing, the withdrawals, everything. Mostly, when I was on pills, what I would experience would be, like I said, diarrhea, hot and cold sweats. It would start off with yawning and I was tearing up. I would not able to sleep. Sleeping was a joke. But, the worst part about it, to me, was the restless legs.

It made me want to put a bullet in my brain. I pierced my calf with one of those pins: really long pins, safety pin type thing, but the really big ones. Yeah, I pierced my calf because I was tired of feeling the way I felt. My legs were just crazy and I'd get so angry. My emotions were all over the place. Up and down, back and forth. I was angry for so long cause I was stuck. You know, I knew who I wanted to be. I was so frustrated because at 16 years of age, I had so much more than I even do right now. You know, I had dreams and I was going to fulfill them and I was living this life that I shouldn't have.

Kimber Lynne: The darkest moment that you finally said, "Come get me now. Come save me. It's now. Pick me up now. My choice." When did that happen for you and what happened to make you get help?

Chayne: What happened was this was last summer, last June, me and my mother had been using together for about four months. We were drug buddies, I guess. We had totally isolated ourselves from everyone else, and we were just using. Drugs were killing a lot of people where I'm from, and we were burying a lot of people I knew. They were dropping like flies every day.

Me and mom were in the car one day, and we were just wondering when it was going to be our turn, if it was going to be her, if it was going to be me and I realized that we were going to die from this. In that moment, it clicked that I didn't want to die. I wanted to live now. And it was a pretty profound moment that for about an hour we just sat in the car holding each other crying and we made the phone call to Mobile Crisis and that we wanted to go to detox. They came to us within an hour and did assessments on us and the next day they had us in a detox.

Kimber Lynne: That's fantastic. So, does advertising work for addicts? "Call this number. If you need addiction help, call this number." Does it help? What helps?

Chayne: For me, what helped with me was word of mouth. Well, the biggest thing was somebody told me that number to call, so I knew to call that number when I wanted help, and I did. I went to detox and I went to detox two more times after that, but I got out and seeing a friend of mine that was in the addiction with me a year prior and seeing how he had changed his life really amazed me. It really gave me hope that if he could do it, I can do it too and so I started hanging real tight with him and learning how he did it and we're still hanging tight today.

Kimber Lynne: Is it fair to say that most addicts don't want to be addicts?

Chayne: Yes. I think so. I don't think anyone would choose to live this life, but it's when you're in that place, it feels like that's all there is. It feels like there's no other way and when you don't know a better way, you're going to keep on doing what you've always done. As soon as the pain gets more than the fear of asking for help, you'll step out of that cycle. You'll try something different and ask for help.

Kimber Lynne: Last question.

Chayne: Yes, ma'am.

Kimber Lynne: I don't know if there's an answer to this, but I'm going to ask it. I hear this, "I started for fun, just kind of messing around wanted to have a good time, wanted to fit in. I was depressed," things like that. Sound familiar?

Chayne: Yes, ma'am.

Kimber Lynne: And then I hear, "Then I went here and there was no going back." Is "here" a specific drug, or can it be multiple drugs, or is it like once you hit cocaine, there's no turning back? Once you hit heroin, there is no turning back? Is there a specific drug? If someone's reading this and they're like, "I'm messing around with this. I'm smoking pot. I'm doing this. I'm doing that," and then they hear, someone say, "I can promise you, If you do this drug or if you shoot up, your life is ruined for sure, because I'm an addict. I'm telling you this." Is there a drug that once you hit that line, there is no turning back?

Chayne: I don't know if there's a specific drug because everyone is different. I've seen people who just drink and they hit that line where they thought there was no turning back. Same thing with cocaine. The same thing with heroin. I think it's once you wake up in the morning and that's the first thing on your mind and you feel like you need that to function to get through the day, then you've crossed the line that you're going to need some help to get back from.

Jill: Well, I can say this for an addict in recovery. It is a struggle every single day of my life to stay clean. I don't think that people who have never been through addiction or don't have anyone that they know personally that have been through it, I don't think they realize that when you see a recovering addict standing in front of you, they said, "I've been clean for a year, a day, two months, what have you," they're a miracle. Because, like you say, it's right in front of me.

I mean absolutely, I can be approached at a gas station, "Hey, are you looking for anything? I have this." And, just as easily, there's certain areas in my town that I could go, that I know that it would be right there. That hangs over my head every single day as an addict, but I have a choice now. Now I have a choice.

9

LISTEN, LEARN AND MOST OF ALL – LOVE

▲▲▲

"Any parent, who has a child that's using, they're suffering. They're in a lot of pain."

▲▲▲

When our children are young, we are very attentive. We understand that they cannot survive without us. As parents, it is our responsibility to do everything for them. As they become teenagers, we step back, allowing them to grow and mature and make mistakes so they will learn. At the same time, we become involved in our careers, trying to provide for the family, trying to prepare to send them off to college. It is hard to imagine that a child who is successful in the classroom or achieving athletically or musically is somehow feeling less than sufficient – feeling insecure, hurting in such a way that they are looking to escape the everyday challenges of life. Trying to fit in and believing that altering their being is the ticket to popularity and happiness. I read a mother's story about her son who overdosed not too long ago. These stories are becoming way too prevalent on the internet and in individual support groups on social media. Basically, her son was just that, popular, smart, good looking, and a pretty good athlete.

She expressed that in certain sports, the use of opioids is widespread. Shocking? We, as parents, do not have the education nor the tools to deal with the early onset and full-blown signs of addiction.

> *Kimber Lynne:* If parents are not going to enable but they have their eyes on their loved one, what are they looking for? Why are they missing it? How are they so far detached from their children that they can't see the different mood swings? You hear the classic stuff, but other things are going on that they're missing. What do you think they need to look for specifically?
>
> *Jill:* I think there is pain. I mean, I know that away from the telltale signs of me hanging out with so and so and coming home late and them finding blunt wrappers in my trunk, I wish they saw the pain that I was in as a teen. If they could've addressed that pain, my parents, I love them to death! My parents were very focused on, well, what she's doing to me, what I was doing to them, what she's doing to the family. She's hurting the family. She's hurting us. She's hurting us financially. She's hurting our reputation. But, they didn't stop to see what all the focus should've been on? The fact that I was hurting. Any parent who has a child that's using, they're suffering. They're in a lot of pain.
>
> *Marie:* For me, I always felt different, growing up, even at an early age. I could tell that there was something just a little

different, even though I didn't play the shy girl inside of me. I had so many insecurities. I wasn't the prettiest or the smartest. I was told a lot of these things by family members as well. And so, I had that instilled in my head.

▲ ▲ ▲

Some have been at this addiction thing with a loved one for a very long time. Many are just beginning the journey. As you put one step in front of the other, you need to know the three C's: I didn't cause it, I can't control it, and I can't cure it.

This is where the faith in God and the love comes in. I remember praying and praying that there would be an easy solution to the problem we were facing. So very many times, I would awake in the middle of the night, wondering where my child was. Were they ok? Would I get the call? If you are in this, then you know which call! After all, it's the power of the drug that is calling out for the addict to use. The brain is telling the addict the body needs this to get back to what you and I believe is normal. After all, what is normal, really? In the beginning, there was anger and there were loud voices trying to get the point across that we were extremely unhappy with the life they were leading. Controversy, anger, elevated voices just made the problem at hand worse.

Anxiety levels intensified. Looking back, we just pushed him to use and probably use more. The time came where we felt helpless, and frankly, we were tired. This was when we moved into the outpouring of love. Daily texts of "I Love You." More texts, saying how much we believe in him or something as simple as "thinking about you." There were no more loud voices and the anger was suppressed. There was no more enabling as by now; I knew that the $20 he needed for a little bit of gas or a meal could be the $20 used to buy the deadly mix of heroin that could kill him. I didn't want to be responsible for that.

It's important once you get to this point, to still be involved as much as they will let you without giving money, transportation, etc. If their world is not rocked, and they are comfortable in their current environment, they will keep on doing what they have been doing. Why, because they haven't experienced the consequences of using. You have to be strong. Oh, it's not easy. Every family is different, and love is projected differently in each unit. I can tell you that LOVE is a powerful instrument to reach someone who is broken and addicted to something that renders them powerless. I was on a radio talk show last week talking about the interviews I had captured over two years and a caller wanted to know when to seek help for a loved one that they know is using. My answer is quite subjective and it is not the case all the time; however, I said you have to listen. Listen for the cry out for help. Once you have cut off the money and other comforts of life, then the addiction will start to unravel their life. Have you heard the saying "rock bottom"? Again, everyone's position on what is rock bottom is very different, but when they get closer to their "rock bottom," there will be one of two things. It's either going to be an accidental overdose or a cry for help because they don't want to live this way anymore. I can speak from experience that it can happen.

And when it does, you have to act immediately. Not next week or three days from the cry, but right when it happens. Be prepared ahead of time that your world will be rocked for 24-48 hours as you try to get them placed in a treatment center. Do research in your community. Find your options. Talk to your community and government leaders because trust me, they know what is going on and can help you find the right place for your loved one. If there is no insurance, they may qualify for Medicaid. There are free rehabilitation centers. It is worth every minute you spend to be in front of the cry for help when the time comes and hopefully it will. When this call comes the addict is at their weakest point in their brokenness and will go without a fight to a facility. Be prepared that the cry for help could come at any hour. Don't hesitate. In my situation, we delivered our child 6 hours away at three in the morning.

I was relieved but very naive about what it was going to take to get the addiction under control. Not cured but manageable. Let's just get into a 28-day program and get the tools needed to move on. Step one accomplished. Step two was something I hadn't anticipated and really wasn't prepared to tackle; relapse.

Twenty-eight days didn't work. And now I know that it doesn't work for those who are addicted to opioids. I wish someone could have prepared me for what was to come. Through it all, we maintained our love for our child and never once judged how they ended up in this place in their life. It took about two years before he was ready to leave the recovery house and enter life as he once knew it. One of the most significant rewards came in a phone call about a year into the recovery process. Our child was in recovery with an athlete from a large University who was also on the Dean's list. Good looking, smart, and athletically superior but suffering from the same disease as my child. They had a lot in common and my son shared a few dinners with the friend's family. My child understood that the mother was struggling with her child's addiction and after one of those dinners, I received a call. My child explained the dynamics of the family and little bit about how the friend came to be in the same recovery house and wanted to know if I would feel comfortable calling the mother to explain unconditional love. That phone call made me realize that somewhere in this horrific journey, my husband and I did something right even though looking back, it felt so wrong. Wow, he wants me to comfort this woman and tell her that everything would be alright or at least let her know that she needed to continue to love and believe in the recovery. I called her the next day and spend over an hour on the phone, welcoming her story and feeling her pain. I've said it before; once you are dealing with full-blown addiction, the story becomes all too familiar with different names and cities. She, like many of us, or I may say all of us, was keeping her pain locked up in a terrible secret. She was imploding and avoiding social scenes, as to not disclose her child's addiction. What would their friends think? How would this affect she and her husband's career? How would it impact her other children? I could tell she was broken and was happy to be able to unload to a fellow parent of an addict, an addict she had shared meals with several times. She felt safe telling the details of her journey and the pain it had caused.

You will find that once you can talk about it openly, you will begin to free yourself from some of the pain you have been carrying. If you are judged by what happened in your home, with your family, then you will realize those people don't belong in your life, anymore. Start today by silencing the stigma. Talk it out and learn what you can about addiction so that you can be a part of a successful recovery plan for your loved one. I think it's important to understand that "addicts don't want to be addicts"! One hundred percent of the recovered addicts I interviewed confessed that once they became addicted, they didn't know how to get out of using.

10

FINDING HOPE IN OTHER'S SUCCESS

▲▲▲

"I wanted to become the daughter that my parents had always prayed for and you know, the family member that everyone didn't have to worry about."

▲▲▲

Kimber Lynne: You see the future. I see it in you. I can see that you now realize, you don't need that.

Diane: Yeah. It's incredible how fast, once you get sober, how fast your life changes for the better. You know, I spent a decade in hell. I mean, hell. I mean, hell. You know I really probably could go on all day with the shit that I've done and, you know, everything that I've experienced. But, today, I'd rather talk about what I'm going to do, which is I'm going to go back to school. My entire life, my dream was to be a psychiatrist. I've always wanted to help people. All my friends always came to me for advice. Always. So, I was like; I should get paid for this. But, today, I'm going to go to school to be a substance abuse counselor, because I want to help people just like me.

Marie: It's going to be one of the hardest things that you ever have to do and maintaining sobriety and clean time is even harder; you work at yourself every single day. You don't get complacent or bored. That's what will kill you. That'll take you right back to where you just were. Change your life because you can do it. There's always somebody out there willing to help. It's just around the corner. It's not hard to find. The road that you take using drugs will lead to your death. If it's alcohol, it's a slow death. Drugs, like I said, will get you there fast. Reach out to somebody even if you're not sure if you are ready yet, just reach out – talk to somebody – ask for help. Not everybody's going to judge you. There are people out there who are willing to do what they need to do to help anyone. For me? I want to eventually be a therapist and I want to work in this field. And if I can just reach one person even if that one person is saving myself for the rest of my life, I've done something. I've done something for me. I've done something for this world and for this community. Just try, just try it.

Wayne: I feel like I've been forgiven. I just thought that's why I believe I need to get involved in the community to spread the message. It's kind of funny that actually, my sponsee, that I used to sell drugs to a year and a half ago was sharing that I was in his driveway selling drugs and using drugs with him, and now I am in his driveway picking him up to go to a meeting. So, change is possible. I do believe that people can change. They just have to be honest. They need to have a willingness and surrender. I can no longer live like this. I can no longer do this, and I am worthy, and I do deserve better in life, and that's where I am today. It's awesome.

Michelle: I believe that once people start realizing, that they have had the strength inside of them this whole time to overcome this demon. I guess you could call it a demon of the darkness. Whatever you refer to your addiction as it is. I don't know that I could have done it without the 12-step program of Alcoholics Anonymous and Narcotics Anonymous. They taught me how to live again as an adult and as a productive member of society. It's just been a lot of years of learning experience after learning experience and usually always having to somehow take the hardest way possible. Ultimately, knowing that this is not my purpose. I was meant to do something in this life. That is good. And I was meant to leave something behind that is good. I wanted to become the daughter that my parents had always prayed for and the family member that everyone didn't have to worry about and I just really wanted my friends and family to feel content. But all of these feelings came after waking up from the nightmare, the nightmare that was my addiction.

Chayne: Rehab is a good place to get knowledge for the disease, and that's what an addict needs to recover. They need self-knowledge about what they're dealing with. But you're not going to get clean unless you really want it. You can go to 10 years' worth of rehabs and if you don't want it for yourself, then you're going to continue to use.

▲▲▲

If you are like the thousands of us who are dealing with addiction, then you probably have tirelessly worked the internet to find information and hope. I am amazed at the social media groups from all over the country that provide support. I have taken a few paragraphs that have been shared so that you know that this disease of addiction can be overcome.

(SOCIAL MEDIA POST)
Throughout the years, we found a life of addiction together. We both had pain we couldn't cope with and trauma we never addressed. Long nights of liquor blackouts consumed us. Then he progressed down a different path than I did. And I separated myself from the world. Both unified in addiction- but distant from each other. My overdose and experience with God led me to a path of recovery. His six overdoses led him further into the depths of this hell we call addiction. I thought, "I can save him since I know the way out." But I couldn't. I begged him, pleaded with him. It didn't matter. So, I stepped back after ten years and focused on myself. I realized I couldn't save him.
And I slept. And I ate. And I felt. All of the things I couldn't do before I let go.

About a month later, Zack calls me.
"I want to go to rehab. I don't want to do this anymore" He decided to save himself; something I couldn't do. And he DID. Today we're both in recovery by the grace of God. We thrive. We love. We've come together as a force to show those who are lost in addiction that there is a way out.
There is. We are proof. Recovery is possible- don't for a second believe it's not.

Kimber Lynne

(SOCIAL MEDIA POST)
Ask your Dr. for a patch called Butrans. IT WORKS. I was on opioids for seven years and didn't know HOW to get off, even though I was desperate to. Get on the patch and ween off. It completely works! Trust me, I never in a million years thought I would be able to be off those. It does have Saboxone in it.

(SOCIAL MEDIA POST)
We do recover. I was a heroin addict shooting up I'm Camden, NJ. I was in a coma from septic shock and endocarditis. I have flat-lined, overdosed and I was the stereotypical junkie. I got clean, married my wife, we adopted a beautiful little girl (THROUGH CHILD PROTECTIVE SERVICES WE GOT OUR DAUGHTER!) and we just bought a beautiful home. YOU CAN DO IT!!!!!!

(SOCIAL MEDIA POST)
Asking for prayers for my son. My husband and I stopped enabling him and as hard as it has been let him venture the path he chose. He came to me today, said he needed help and asked me to take him to the VA. They are sending him through intense rehab. Just left him and thanking God for prayers answered. I know he has a long way to go but I know with God all things are possible. Thanks so much!

(SOCIAL MEDIA POST)
Today, even when I'm not happy, I am? If you get that, it's confusing, but even my good days in addiction ain't half as terrible as my bad days in recovery. So, I always try and remember that! Also, I don't regret my past, nor do I wish to

shut the door on it. I have acceptance of it, and I'm using it for good. I've learned from it and have moved on guilt-free!

Wow, this is just amazing. I've done a lot of work to get thus far, didn't come easy, but more comfortable than being in active addiction. I hate when people say recovery is hard; yes, it's hard, but living life homeless and trying to find your next high, so you don't get sick is HARD. Today, I personally know peace and have serenity. I'm no longer fighting with my mom and dad every day, no longer waking up to the drama or have people banging on my door looking for dope. I now realize how my story can benefit others, and that's one of my biggest purposes today! To inspire and help others recover from the things I never thought I would or could. I don't feel like I'm useless, and I've stopped that self-pity party. NOW this is a huge one for me; I've lost complete interest in that lifestyle.

▲ ▲ ▲

This journey of recovery for my son and our family has not been easy. I had to learn to be honest with myself, accept my emotions for what they are, face the darkness of the past and learn the future is more important than the past. I'd be lying to you if I said I had the answer to beating addiction. Is there a solid solution and a detailed path that works for everyone? Absolutely not! Addiction is like every other disease that requires self-discipline, and many diseases have to be controlled by medications. Mental illness for instance, or heart disease or diabetes, all of which are prescribed medicines to keep the disease manageable. I have also come to realize that everyone who has experience with addiction will give you their formula to what has to happen in order to overcome the addiction. You have to find what works for you or your loved one. No one is wrong in what they believe because for them what they did worked. Here are some of the things that I have been told in my two years of interviewing that you may want to research.

Let's begin with the twelve-step approach AA, which was founded by Bill Wilson and his physician, Doctor Bob Smith in 1935. In 1939, Wilson published a text entitled Alcoholics Anonymous, which outlined the organization's methods and philosophy. We know it today as the 12 Steps of recovery. AA gives men and women a safe environment to share their experiences and gain encouragement from others who are in recovery from alcoholism, and it provides a means to help maintain sobriety. The notion centers around the belief that alcoholism is an illness that can be managed, but not controlled. These are the twelve steps that are being used and followed by many enjoying recovery from addiction. (www.hazeldenbettyford.org)

> Step 1: We admitted we were powerless over alcohol that our lives had become unmanageable
> Step 2: Came to believe that a Power greater than ourselves could restore us to sanity
> Step 3: Made a decision to turn our will and our lives over to the care of God as we understood Him
> Step 4: Made a searching and fearless moral inventory of ourselves
> Step 5: Admitted to God, to our self, and to another human being the exact nature of our wrongs
> Step 6: Were entirely ready to have God remove all these defects of character

Step 7: Humbly asked Him to remove our shortcomings
Step 8: Made a list of all persons we had harmed and became willing to make amends to them all
Step 9: Made direct amends to such people wherever possible, except when to do so would injure them or others
Step 10: Continued to take personal inventory and when we were wrong promptly admitted it
Step 11: Sought through prayer and meditation to improve our conscious contact with God, as we understood Him, praying only for knowledge of His will for us and the power to carry that out
Step 12: Having had a spiritual awakening as the result of these Steps, we tried to carry this message to alcoholics, and to practice these principles in all our affairs

According to Wikipedia, Narcotics Anonymous (NA) describes itself as a "nonprofit fellowship or society of men and women for whom drugs had become a major problem." As of May 2018, there were more than 70,000 NA meetings in 144 countries.

Individuals who are suffering relinquish to a higher power. For many, this is God. For others, it is a spiritual connection that allows them to lean not on their own understanding. Most of the rehabilitation treatment centers require the 12-step approach because it has proven effective in the recovery process.

For Opioid addiction, there are methods of aiding in the recovery process. Many of the addicts that I interviewed said they needed help medically to ween off of opioids. This entails being monitored daily or monthly with a prescribed approach of helping with the detoxification of opioid addiction. One of these is "Methadone," which is a synthetic analgesic drug that is similar to morphine in its effects but longer acting. Methadone reduces withdrawal symptoms in people addicted to heroin or other narcotic drugs without causing the "high."

Another is known as "Saboxone." Suboxone is a prescription medication that combines buprenorphine and naloxone. It is used to treat opioid addiction. Buprenorphine belongs to a class of drugs called opioid partial agonists, which help relieve symptoms of opiate withdrawal.

I hired a guy to power wash my house last year, and he asked about the t-shirt I was wearing that was in support of a local non-profit championing recovery from opioid addiction. He was proud to share that he was in active recovery from a Heroin addiction. I became vested, as I was deep into the interview process for my documentary, so I asked him how he was doing and why was he successful? He shared that he was on a Vivitrol program down in the county, administered by a medical doctor. Vivitrol is a once-monthly injection that blocks opioid receptors in the brain for one month at a time, helping patients to prevent relapse to opioid dependence. The other substitute, I was introduced to during the interview process was Kratom. This supplement is getting a lot of discussion among the DEA and the general public. Again, I could write a whole book just on Kratom. I only mention it to alert you that it's out there and some believe it works like some of the other antigens. Kratom is believed to act on opioid receptors and help with withdrawals producing sedation, pleasure, and decreased pain, especially when users consume large amounts of the plant. There is some concern over the efficacy of its claim, as it relates to opiates, as well as safety.

I will leave you with this. Education about the disease of addiction is imperative to understanding what you or your loved one is going through. Keep an open mind throughout the journey. Don't ever give up because there are many stories of successful recoveries. Remain hopeful and love unconditionally. Lean on others to help you and don't let your mind take you to dark places. I am hopeful and encouraged that eyes are opened and that the government is listening and reacting with new measures to change the opioid crisis in America.